# How to Start, Operate and Fund a Non-Profit Mental Health and Substance Abuse Organization

*With special sections on Primary Care and Pharmacotherapy*

by

Matt Hamilton, MBA, Ph.D.

1663 LIBERTY DRIVE, SUITE 200
BLOOMINGTON, INDIANA 47403
(800) 839-8640
WWW.AUTHORHOUSE.COM

*This book is a work of non-fiction. Unless otherwise noted, the author and the publisher make no explicit guarantees as to the accuracy of the information contained in this book and in some cases, names of people and places have been altered to protect their privacy.*

*© 2005 Matt Hamilton, MBA, Ph.D.. All Rights Reserved.*

*No part of this book may be reproduced, stored in a retrieval system, or transmitted by any means without the written permission of the author.*

*First published by AuthorHouse 04/14/05*

*ISBN: 1-4208-2104-0 (sc)*

*Library of Congress Control Number: 2004195555*

*Printed in the United States of America*
*Bloomington, Indiana*

*This book is printed on acid-free paper.*

For

Vanessa, Kristen, Danielle & Jordan

Family is what matters most of all…

# Preface

This book is intended to provide a clear and comprehensive step-by-step operating and compliance guide for counselors, therapists, physicians, community health agencies, mental health and substance abuse providers within a not-for-profit organization environment. Included within this book, you'll find ready to use technical policy and procedure manuals, business plan designs, physician employment agreements and operational grant funding proposals, all of which are easily customizable to fit your specific organizational design and capabilities. Moreover, those providers that are currently offering counseling and/or substance abuse services will find a fully functional model in which to launch an integrated healthcare facility that is capable of delivering primary care with or without pharmacotherapy services.

While reading this book you must keep in mind that there are a lot of moving parts when it comes to starting and operating your own healthcare organization. Thus, this text is designed to move you logically along the disparate and confusing processes of incorporation, licensing, funding, program development, grant writing, business plan development, staff recruitment and retention, accounting, budgeting, marketing and community development. Historically, many people who start their own organization do not have a lot of money in which to hire top consultants, attorneys, accountants and public relation firms. Therefore, one of the main objectives of this book is to guide you systematically and methodically through these fundamental processes that will enable you to learn to do the bulk of the grunt work yourself that's necessary to create and sustain a strong viable agency. Furthermore, the specific examples included in this text will allow you to minimize your cash outlays for certain consultants and outsource contractors. However, certain consultants such as accountants and attorneys may be necessary to put the last touches on certain facets of your business model.

The goal of this book is to provide valuable knowledge to those of you who have decided that you are committed to pursuing your dream of providing healthcare services within your community, yet, lack the necessary knowledge of available resources needed to complete your goals. Additionally, this book is designed to improve your ability to interact successfully with local and Federal health departments, local and Federal funding sources and private organizations interested in collaborating with unique healthcare providers.

This exceptional book provides an expansive blueprint of real life information that can be put to use immediately and effectively. In fact, the technical information contained in this text is so detailed that you can create your organization in as little as 24 hours. And, most importantly, the data contained in this volume is based upon years of comprehensive knowledge. Yet, it is written at a level that is designed to be understandable by the novice behavioral healthcare entrepreneur. Plus, for established behavioral healthcare providers this book includes detailed sections designed to enhance day-to-day operations by upgrading and stabilizing your current service delivery capabilities. The flow of information has been very carefully chronicled to ensure that essential processes and structures are considered and brought to your attention early on in the process. Again, the goal is to minimize your overall financial outlays and to avoid unnecessary time consumption. However, running an organization is not easy and you have to be committed to becoming successful.

Outlined within this text you will find a wealth of information that has been designed to allow you to operate your new organization in a cost-effective manner, and to be as productive as possible with limited resources at your disposal. The section on revenue should be particularly beneficial for the hundreds of organizations that are currently in the process of redesigning their operations with the expectation of reigniting positive growth and curbing costs. In addition, there is a special pharmacotherapy section that contains enough detailed information needed to start, introduce, or enhance the use of pharmaceutical detoxification and maintenance.

Lastly, I invite your thoughtful comments regarding this book. Also, suggestions for corrections or other contributions should be forwarded directly to me for review. All formally acknowledged contributions will be used in the next edition.

Matthew Hamilton, MBA, Ph.D.
mhamilton@marlinone.com

# Table of Contents

Preface ................................................................................. vii

Chapter 1 Introduction ........................................................... 1
    Cash Flow ........................................................................ 2

Chapter 2 Philosophy .............................................................. 4
    Business Acumen ............................................................. 4

Chapter 3 Communication ...................................................... 6
    Communicate Honestly ................................................... 6
    Loyalty and Commitment ................................................ 7
    Sharing Information ........................................................ 8
    Normal Reaction ............................................................. 9

Chapter 4 Corporation Structure ........................................... 10
    The 501(c)(3) ................................................................ 10
    Employer Identification Number .................................. 11
    Diversification ............................................................... 12
    Financial Storms ........................................................... 12

Chapter 5 Board of Directors ................................................ 15
    Façades of Authority .................................................... 15
    Experiential Repertoire ................................................. 16
    Amicable Relationships ................................................ 17
    Kindred ......................................................................... 18
    Channeling ................................................................... 19

Chapter 6 Business Plan ....................................................... 20
    Fine Toothcomb ........................................................... 20
    How Bankers Think ...................................................... 21
    Formats For Business Plans ......................................... 22
    Executive Summary ..................................................... 22
    Current Marketing Situation ......................................... 23
    Opportunities and Issues Analysis ............................... 23

|  |  |
|---|---|
| Objectives | 24 |
| Marketing Strategy | 24 |
| Ecosystem | 25 |
| Budget | 25 |
| FTE | 26 |
| Controls | 27 |

**Chapter 7 Revenue** ...................................................................40
- Unrestricted Money ..........................................................40
- Restricted Money ..............................................................41
- Commingling Funds ..........................................................42
- Medical Doctors ................................................................43
- Physicians Understand .....................................................44
- Closing Enrollment ............................................................45

**Chapter 8 Grants** ......................................................................47
- Community Development Block Grants (CDBG) .......47
- Technical Assistance .........................................................49
- Positive Revenue Management .....................................50
- State Grant Funding ..........................................................51
- Hiring Grant Writers ..........................................................56
- Ongoing Submission ........................................................57
- Tight Niche Group ............................................................58
- Experiential Reservoir ......................................................59

**Chapter 9 Loans** ........................................................................74
- Economic Development ..................................................74
- Leverage Cash ...................................................................75
- Personal Nature .................................................................76

**Chapter 10 Finance and Accounting** ...................................78
- Audited Financial Statement ..........................................78
- Dollars and Sense .............................................................79
- Dollar for Dollar .................................................................79
- Financial Integrity .............................................................82
- Financial Health ................................................................83

Chapter 11 Marketing ................................................................99
    Right Of Entry ..................................................................99
    Airspace .........................................................................100
    In-house Marketing .......................................................101
    Pick Up The Phone .......................................................102
    Fee for Service ..............................................................104
    Employee Assistance Services ......................................105
    Drug and Alcohol Testing Services ..............................106

Chapter 12 Staffing ..................................................................116
    Paid Employees ............................................................116
    Counseling And Psychotherapy .....................................117
    Volunteers .....................................................................117
    Physician Recruiting – *Making the case for a Visa in a Health Profession Shortage Area* ...............................*119*
    H-1B1 ............................................................................119
    Health Profession Shortage Area ..................................121
    Labor Attestation ..........................................................123
    Licensure Board ............................................................139
    Country Of Expatriate Origin .......................................142
    Needs Analysis .............................................................143
    Census Track ................................................................144
    Timetable ......................................................................144
    State Approves ..............................................................154

Chapter 13 Psychotherapy and Counseling ...........................155
    Path of Responsibility ..................................................155

Chapter 14 Creating Primary Care with Pharmacotherapy
    Program ........................................................................247
    New Driver ...................................................................247
    Significance of the Psychiatrist ....................................248
    Disjointed Treatment ....................................................249
    Integrated Health Delivery System ...............................250
    Catalyst For Compliance ..............................................251
    Facility License ............................................................252
    Wide-Ranging Guide ....................................................254

> Handling Narcotics ..................................................... 255

Chapter 15 Organization Command and Control ........................ 274
> SWOT ............................................................................ 274
> Just Do Yourself A Favor ............................................... 275
> Make Adjustments ......................................................... 276

Summary For Directors Only ................................................... 287

Index ......................................................................................... 289

# Chapter 1
# Introduction

Planning to start or change the way in which an organization operates takes a great deal of thought and energy. And, if you don't have the knowledge—a great deal of money. Throughout the United States there are a lot of practitioners that are getting ready to obtain their licenses to become independent providers, physicians who are treating a great number of comorbid patients in their private practices, and healthcare agencies that just can't seem to grow, or sustain positive growth. Unfortunately, those of you who had previously made up your minds to start up your very own organization have at some point found out that you would have to pay consultants and grant writers thousands of dollars before you could get started. However, the reality for most people is that they do not have ready access to a great deal of cash. In general, what usually happens is that most people drop the whole idea and resume their everyday activities.

There have been many books written on how to start up various businesses, yet, not one of them was designed for healthcare providers; in particular, mental health, substance abuse and primary care. The goal of this book is to put all of the relevant facts and workable information regarding this type of business in one place. Thus, providing you the opportunity to forgo deep financial outlays of cash, and to teach you how to use as little of your own money as possible to make your project successful. As you read through this book please remember that the most important problem with operating a non-profit is that they generally run like non-profits. Thus, the primary focus of this book is to teach you to operate your company as though it is a for-profit entity. The end result will be a strong and well ran organization that will be able to expand and grow even during times when your peers are floundering in the same market.

## Cash Flow

The survival of a non-profit organization just as the continued existence of a for-profit business depends solely upon cash. Cash flow is often non-existent with many start-ups. Daily operations such as the telephone, rent, electric, insurance and payroll consume most of the revenue before it is even generated. One of the most fundamental concepts in healthcare that is most often overlooked and underestimated is the concept of "patient service financing." In other words, the provider is the root financier of a particular service for the client, or patient. Sure, the insurance company pays the bill once it is submitted and reviewed, but, in the meantime the organization has to keep the phones and lights turned on. Thus, your organization in effect becomes a lender as you are extending credit to the consumer for a specified amount of time. The challenge is that you have to learn how to have more money coming in than you do have going back out.

In short, if you cannot sustain constant cash flow, and predict revenue with accuracy then your organization will be in constant turmoil, and will always be a going concern, which in accounting language means that you are a financial risk and that your organization can close up shop in the middle of the night. So, then the fundamental question becomes, "How can you go from zero to sixty without gas?"

# Chapter 2
# Philosophy

As was noted earlier, perhaps the most important concept to remember when developing an operating philosophy is that the organization should be ran like a for profit business. Many of today's healthcare organizations face a phenomenon called "profitless growth." For many years, the main emphasis of an organization was to grow and grow and grow. However, growth may not always be a good thing. In fact, larger organizations find it very difficult to stay afloat during times of poor revenue flow. Likewise, where it pertains to controlling costs and stabilizing revenue streams large companies must engage in drastic remedies because their cash flow needs are so enormous. Thus, it becomes quite imperative that you develop a positive cash flow that exceeds your needs without delay.

## Business Acumen

How does this relate to philosophy? Many people that consider starting a non-profit are primarily undertaking this pursuit for altruistic reasons. And while this notion is a commendable one, you must keep in mind that all of the people who join your cause, including those that come to rely on your timely services will demand that you deliver upon all of your promises each and every day. The fundamental lesson to be learned here is that you must not run this business with your heart. The agency's operations must be run with keen business acumen. Yet, that is not to say that you must forsake the reasons that brought you thus far, but you must have professional managers working along side you in order to be successful. Sure, there are going to be times when matters of the heart will prevail in a given situation. Yet, if you're a good director, someday even your most hardened managers will become "soft" hearted and they'll assist you in finding sound financial opportunities to make your altruistic dreams a reality.

# Chapter 3
# Communication

The single most important tool that a manager has is communication. Thus, whenever there is an impending crisis facing the organization you must learn to always communicate with your employees both honestly and truthfully. This above board way of doing business will help you to gain their help and support should the organization ever experience any difficult times. This is critical in that there are going to be days in the beginning when cash on hand is going to equal zero. Nevertheless, for the most part this scenario can be avoided with careful financial planning and good strategic decision-making. On the other hand, you must prepare for the unexpected during the good times. For example, you have to ask yourself the question, "What will I do if I can't make payroll on time this pay period?" "Do I tell anyone?" And, "If I do—what exactly will I say?"

## Communicate Honestly

Unfortunately, many employees find out that there is a problem when their checks begin to bounce, or someone catches the office manager slipping away into a conference room coming out only to inform the congregation of a crisis. This is a commonplace example, and regrettably, this scenario has been a trend in recent years for many organizations. Sadly, the open communication process has become virtually non-existent within many agencies. It is a fact that many administrators have taken the position that the welfare of an employee takes second place to corporate objectives. Organizations that allow its managers to believe that they are not required to communicate honestly with their employees are likely to face retention and hiring difficulties on an ongoing basis.

## Loyalty and Commitment

Building up the employee's self-esteem and nurturing are a part of the job many managers feel will render them ineffective. They often feel that their subordinates will not respect them if they respond in a less than stern manner. The process for changing management's attitude toward the communication process is a foreseeable goal attainable by cooperation, trust and the fostering of greater employee relations. During the process a manager has to be open-minded and willing to accept the change without feeling as though control is lost. In order to win the hearts and minds of those employees that you are going to have to eventually depend upon to keep the organization running, a great sense of loyalty and commitment has to be earned.

Managers can no longer take communication for granted. Employees are now beginning to empower themselves with better education and have progressively become more outspoken than in previous generations. Closing the door on this new breed of employee is no longer acceptable or practical. They demand respect and will not be ignored. Additionally, your employees may also be required to obtain training that will assist them in the process of receiving open communication from your managers. Ultimately, the objective is to permit them to respond without feeling intimidated. If not, this situation will lead to frustration on the part of the employee that eventually results in further breakdown of communication within the work group.

## Sharing Information

Again, there are many ways to prevent this from occurring. First of all management has to guarantee that everyone within the organization has the opportunity to openly communicate his or her feelings without consequence and that everyone is comfortable in doing so. Secondly, all managers must have a genuine interest in developing their own abilities to effectively communicate. And, what you'll find is that down the road this skill will be extremely beneficial should an unexpected revenue shortfall occur—particularly given the erratic nature of grant funding.

To clarify, let's refer back to the payroll example. Whereas, payroll is due on Friday, but you just found out that your primary funding source isn't going to release a check until the following Tuesday. If as a manager you've developed a good team spirit, as well as, a firm sense of trust within your staff then this unforeseeable occurrence should not be a considerable problem. However, if management has a historical policy of not sharing information, and now the money is not going to be in the bank on time, then it is almost certain that there is going to be an ugly revolt.

## Normal Reaction

It should also be noted that besides communicating to your employees in a timely manner the same could be said for your main funding sources. It is absolutely imperative that you or your designated representatives communicate in a timely manner with all of your financial sources and vendors. Unfortunately, and quite often whenever an agency experiences an abrupt shortfall of cash it becomes very uncomfortable to talk about the subject. The normal reaction is to feel depressed and helpless. However, do not allow your false pride to hinder and hamper your best efforts. Once again, going through and surviving this process will inevitably make you wiser and stronger. The most important thing to remember when talking to your vendors is to not make promises that you can't reasonably keep. Also, when asking for an extension to make a payment, request the time that you really need. Don't make the mistake of asking for two days to come up with the money—when all along you knew that you needed a week. You'll be surprised to find that the vendor would rather receive your payment as agreed to in a week as opposed to becoming disappointed and frustrated when you miss the payment in two days.

# Chapter 4
# Corporation Structure

As you proceed with the process of designing your organization one of the most important business decisions that you'll make is going to be the actual structure of your corporation. The corporate structure that is eventually chosen will determine such things as tax liability and personal responsibility as it relates to doing business in a particular state or commonwealth. However, kept in mind that many organizations who provide mental health, substance abuse and primary care services to community-based residents are most often 501(c)(3) corporations. These non-profit organizations are deemed to be exempt from certain Federal taxes.

## The 501(c)(3)

Now, if it's your intent to pursue grants, and to hold fundraisers to generate additional income for the organization, then the 501(c)(3) designation is absolutely appropriate. In order for an organization to obtain a tax exemption status under section 501(a) of the Internal Revenue Code (IRC) certain basic guidelines have to be met. The IRS specifically relates to this particular entity as a "charitable organization." Federal publication number 557 specifies that the exempt purposes outlined in IRC Section 501(c)(3) should be educational, public safety, charitable, religious, and scientific. Of course, there are other purposes, which can be discovered by examining the full text of that section of the IRC rule. However, the rule goes on to say that the term charitable is used in its commonly acknowledged legal sense and incorporates relief of the poor, distraught or underprivileged people. A charitable organization can also be used for the advancement of religion, improvement of education or science, reduction of the burdens of government, combating community deterioration and juvenile delinquency, erection or maintenance of public buildings, lessening of neighborhood tensions, elimination of prejudice and discrimination and the defense of human and civil rights secured by law.

## Employer Identification Number

The form to use when applying for the charitable organization status is 1023, which can be found online at www.irs.ustreas.gov. And, for assistance and help in filling out this application package you can use IRS Publication 4220 and 557 that is also available on the website. In addition to this application you are going to need an Employer Identification Number (EIN). This number is used to identify your organization when it comes to filing your state and Federal government tax returns, and must be obtained before submitting your exempt status application. Obtaining this number is important for quite a few reasons. For instance, there are several tax returns such as Form 990 "Return of Organizations Exempt from Income Tax" that must be filled out at certain intervals during the year (see the chapter on Accounting). Surely, by now this whole process may seem daunting at first, but, if you are really determined to fulfill your dream of providing services to those individuals and families in the community that need them most, you must begin here first.

## Diversification

As you develop a model for a specific operating structure keep in mind that the non-profit organization can be comprised of many different parts. The entities that are created are called decentralized strategic business units (SBUs). The management of the SBU reports directly to the parent. Furthermore, these entities are legally separate and distinct from the parent corporation. In other words, you can have an integrated behavioral healthcare entity that has a separate housing component such as a group home. The clients that live in that residential home can have their healthcare needs rendered by the parent organization and when they are finished with the appointment they'll return back to the group home. Another example of this type of entity could be that of a food preparation program. Whereas, it may be incorporated as a for-profit entity and its line of business is to provide commercial food services to the public.

## Financial Storms

Why separate the organization? What is the reason for the different corporate designation? The main reason to segregate the organization is "the rule of diversity." This concept will be discussed in detail later in both the accounting and revenue sections. In short, those companies that are prepared to weather unforeseen financial storms are most often successful by ensuring that they have several disparate or separate revenue streams. For instance, all businesses have distinct productivity and revenue cycles that can be for the most part predictive by studying econometric and statistical modeling. These trends are often used as roadmaps for controllers, treasurers and other financial managers in the organization that control investments and cash outlays. The financial savvy executive director is going to want to make sure that cash is coming into the organization year round and on a consistent basis. What's more, you should also be determined to use the unrestricted cash (see accounting) that does come in from various projects to leverage and promote other lucrative revenue streams.

It is important to note that the incorporation process of your company is to be done according to your local laws and statues. This is simply due to the fact there can be several distinctive steps in creating a corporation that vary from state to state such as registering with your state's treasury department. Again, in order to do any of this you will first need to obtain an EIN from the Internal Revenue Service. One of the simpler methods for creating a corporation is to use a company that specializes in preparing a complete package. The myriad of services that these companies can provide include registration of your name, sections of incorporation, by-law assistance, corporate ledger, corporate seal and some will even prepare an EIN application for you as well. As you begin filling out the corporation application it is important that you choose your Board of Directors very carefully and have a clear sense of the expectation that you are going to need from each member. Thus, in the next chapter we will discuss board creation and member development. An entire chapter has been devoted to this subject because a properly functioning board is just that critical, and each selection that is made must be done with deliberate, and very well thought-out intention.

# Chapter 5
# Board of Directors

Many people at this point are often employed at a mental health agency, substance abuse facility, or operating a private medical practice. So, during this time, when the pressure of actually operating an organization has not yet occurred, it is vitally important for you to fill out your corporation application with due diligence, and to begin thinking about how you are going to interact with the group that you have assembled to lead your future organization. And, now that you have decided that you are going to create a not-for-profit structure there are several issues that have to be resolved before you submit your application. First and foremost, you are going to need to elect an independent Board of Directors.

## Façades of Authority

Why do you need Board members other than to fill out your application? Will your board just be a façade of authority put in place, and controlled by the executive director? There are several good reasons to make sure that your board reports directly to the community in which you plan to operate. And, yes, unfortunately there are rubber stamp committees that are dysfunctional, and who are not truly independent of the director. Well, considering that you have high expectations for your new organization and that you want to make it a pillar within your community it is suggested that you avoid those members that you deem are not fully independent of your authority and influence. Assuredly, the most important reason to have an independent Board is to assure outside entities such as the community, local government, funding sources and lending institutions that your organization is trust worthy, founded upon principals and is answerable to it's stakeholders, and not the director. A Board of Directors is a group of talented and caring people who have chosen to donate their expertise and time to your organization.

The list of people that will serve on your board is entirely up to your discretion. But, keep in mind that these members should be a cross section of the community in which you plan to provide your healthcare services. The process of choosing these members should be a momentous and fulfilling journey. In that, this is a unique opportunity to assemble some of the brightest, and most influential members of your community. What type of person are you looking for to sit on your Board? Keeping in mind that both the amount of seats, and time available to hold a position on a particular board are limited—good choices are essential.

## Experiential Repertoire

Preferably, your choice should be an individual that shares your vision as it relates to providing a specific service to a specialized segment of your targeted geographic area. Moreover, it would be a very good idea to include someone that has a keen familiarity with the inner workings of your local government. One of the most common mistakes that organizations make, or fail to address is the quintessential relationship with their local and county governments. Why is this important? It is a well-known fact that the bulk of the funding that goes to a non-profit originates within either the city, or county government. Furthermore, the bulk of all Federal funding is either directly managed, or the application for funding has to be supported by the local government. The competition and the process of applying for available grant dollars is tumultuous, intensive and turbulent. Thus, the whole idea of competitive funding is to ensure that through market forces, the organization with the most creative, and competent ideas to solve public problems will make it to the top. Also, those organizations that are willing to deploy some of their own cash to run a program are viewed in a different light as well. Conversely, there is data that loosely suggests that organizations with sour relationships with local government are generally experiencing a negative cash flow.

## Amicable Relationships

Furthermore, your local government has exclusive control and is solely responsible for the ongoing cash flow of funding for almost all grant projects, real estate donations, and may or may not endorse even directly funded grants from the Federal government. Thus, it is vital that your Board have members that can foster positive and amicable relationships with your local officials.

Another, good choice for a Board member is an attorney. Your corporate attorney can be retired or is currently practicing law. The purpose for choosing an legal expert is that oftentimes many non-profits need to have counsel available to answer specific questions regarding topics such as land and building acquisitions, loan and bonding issues and a host of other commonplace operating functions. This is especially the case when it comes to setting up subsidiaries and decentralized entities.

## Kindred

Should relatives be considered as Board members? There is nothing illegal about putting your brother or mother on the Board. However, perception is reality and appearances are everlasting. In other words, it is very important that your organization be perceived as a solid, no nonsense company. Period. The public has to have a real sense of trust in your ability to safeguard public money and to use donations and fundraising monies for the purposes, and in the spirit for which it was donated. On the other hand, no one is suggesting that your relatives are not worthy people and very responsible, but, in the world of checks and balances funding sources are just more comfortable with autonomous members. Besides, there are other issues to contend with that will surely come up that will be of an emotional nature. For instance, one night a Board meeting may be in session, and one of the invited guests asks a question concerning a finance report that indicates that there are grant funds that need to be allocated immediately. So, subsequently, the Board Treasurer who is your finance officer's father suggests that the money be allocated for a one-time purchase of medical supplies from a new vendor. The funds are unrestricted so a purchase of supplies for an ongoing program seems to be a proper way to make use of this funding. However, the speaker is not in favor of spending this money with a company that is not on the list of your registered vendors. Thus, he requests to have a full detailed analysis of the background of this company before he votes on the matter. Unfortunately, discontent grows like an ivy plant when it comes to questionable expenditures of public money.

## Channeling

The fundamental thought here is not that the money is being spent with a new vendor. The problem that a lot of people will have is that your father is channeling the cash to this particular vendor. Even so, keep in mind that the word channeling was used here on purpose to point out that negative sounding word substitutions such as this will almost always happen when the question of impropriety is brought up. Accordingly, there should be a conscious effort to stay far away from potential conflicts of interest. This is another reason of why it is imperative that you chose Board members that are perceived by the public as having their own separate backgrounds and reference points.

# Chapter 6
# Business Plan

Now that you have your organizational frame work in place the most proven method for accomplishing your goals is by designing a sound business plan. What is a business plan? And, Why do I need it? A business plan is your roadmap for future travels. For example, if you were going to a friends' home for supper and had not been there before, then you would ask for directions. Why? Could it be that you did not want to get lost, and miss the occasion? Or perhaps, you did not want to waste valuable resources like your gas and time. This is the fundamental premise of a business plan. It is a written guide that is put together which spells out specifically just how you are going to achieve the objectives that you have predicted.

## Fine Toothcomb

A good business plan is priceless, and has to be put together in such a way that whoever reads it will clearly and explicitly understand exactly how you are going to accomplish your goals. Again, this plan is going to be used over and over again. It will be requested by almost every entity that you ask for money. The loan officer at your bank will go over this document with a fine toothcomb. The most important questions that your banker will be trying to answer will be: How will the bank be repaid? Where will your revenue come from? Who are your competitors? Who are your Board Members?

On the whole, the most functional business plan model will have several key sections that should tackle and analyze the approach in which you're actually going to run your business. Once again, even though you may be registered as a non-profit business that loan officer is certainly looking at your organization just as if it were a for-profit business. Remember, bankers are first and foremost interested in how you are going to use their money to make enough money to pay your liabilities, and to pay them back, in a timely manner. These folks for obvious reasons are no nonsense in regards to this matter. Yet, make no mistake about this notion that financial institutions believe in community investment, they do, but if you cannot convince them that you know what you are doing, then they will not loan you any money.

## How Bankers Think

All things considered, now that you are aware of the psychology of how bankers think and what they expect, it's going to be up to you to make your case on paper. Besides, you have to keep in mind that when someone picks up your plan for review, this document is going to be a direct reflection on precisely who you are as a planner. The fact of the matter is that a poorly written proposal may not be resurrected or given a second chance. Additionally, given that the person reviewing your documentation has never met you in person, your capabilities and inabilities will become transparent, and obvious to an experienced analyst through your work. Thus, the content and the presentation of the material contained within your plan will have to be polished and accurate. It is paramount that the formulation and the overall structure of the business plan progress in a methodical and organized manner. And, be careful to outline in painstaking detail, the tasks that will need to be accomplished to reach your objectives. Also, remember that the fundamental data supporting your project must be specific and compelling. Bear in mind; do not leave room for speculation.

## Formats For Business Plans

There are a variety of formats for business plans, however, the final version should contain (1) executive summary, (2) current marketing situation, (3) opportunities and issues analysis, (4) objectives, (5) marketing strategy, (6) budget and (7) controls. The overall layout of your plan will depend upon the type of operation that you plan to create, or expand upon.

## Executive Summary

The initial point of contact is the *Executive Summary*, which is designed to introduce your organization, and to give a brief synopsis outlining exactly what it is that you intend to accomplish. The summary should briefly describe your project in no more than one paragraph. In other words, look at this section as your "30 second commercial." It has to contain, the reason for the project, the significant importance and just how much money will be required. All of this information should be briefly and clearly identified. As for the entire business plan, if you do a good job it will be at least 25 to 40 pages in length.

## Current Marketing Situation

The *Current Marketing Situation* defines your intended geographic operating area. In the case of opening a behavioral health center it will contain the relevant demographics of the population that you intend to service. In this section you may also include any extraordinary circumstances that would support or substantiate a particular issue.

## Opportunities and Issues Analysis

The *Opportunities and Issues Analysis* section provides you with the opportunity to look around the horizon. Within this segment of the plan, the organization can detail the environment in which it plans to operate its business. Here in this section, you can elaborate on the things that give you a competitive edge. Also, a full description of your current capabilities must be provided. Or in the case of a startup, the data should drive the tasks that need to be accomplished to acquire your previously stated objectives. This comprehensive analysis of data will assist evaluators to appreciate your projects' future potential.

# Objectives

The next part of the plan directly conveys your *Objectives*. Each point should clearly state the intended upon goal that will be achieved at specific mile markers or points in time. It is essential that synchronization between the objectives and opportunity analysis take place. Note that rough approximations are not acceptable. For instance, if you have stated, "Achieve an encounter rate of 4,300 patients" as a goal and your data only supports a budget for 300 patients, there are going to be questions regarding this serious disconnect of data. The rule to follow is that your plan needs to make sense, and that your intentions coincide with verifiable facts.

# Marketing Strategy

The ideal business plan has a section dedicated to *Marketing Strategy*. Within this section you are going to present the details as to how your services will be presented to the community. And, an essential part of that communication process will be to define the characteristics and behavioral habits of your potential customers. In other words, you have to identify exactly what it is that you believe your customers are seeking. Subsequently, once that has been achieved you can then research the most common pathways of prior acquisition of those services. In addition, this piece will contain all of the competitive intelligence information that you have assembled on your competitors. It is extremely important that you know whom you are going to be competing against and their various capabilities.

## Ecosystem

The ecosystem that you are going to become a part of has many different types of providers, and they each have their own different idiosyncrasies. Since your resources at this point will have to be used with great precision, it is important to discuss the concept of "economy of scale." This simply refers to the notion that the more your organization performs a certain task the more efficient you become as a result. Many organizations strive for this level of existence due to the fact that they have become proficient and are now performing an operation for minimal costs. Whereas, a new competitor in the market is going to have to go through the process of learning and subsequently making costly financial mistakes. This experiential advantage, or economy of scale will ultimately enable you to remain well ahead of the pack when it comes to market share and profitability. In fact, there will be fewer competitors in the market as a direct result of your proficiency.

## Budget

Now that you have a firm plan in place, the next question will be how much is this all going to cost. In the *Budget* section is where you are going to identify all of the costs associated with running your business. The budget is a financial roadmap that essentially spells out the expenditures necessary to accomplish your goals and objectives. The components of the budget include revenue and expenses such as staffing and supply costs. The usual time period for a budget is generally one year. However, there are some grants that may request a budget for a shorter, or longer period of time. Typically, labor is one of the most costly expenses that an organization has to support. Thus, you must be specific as to how many positions that you are going to require to operate effectively.

## FTE

The traditional employee on a healthcare budget is listed as a full time equivalent (FTE) and relates to just one position. One FTE can be designated to represent a traditional 40-hour workweek, or 2080 hours per year. The time breakdown can be as follows: 80 hours bi-weekly, 160 hours for 4 weeks, or 52 weeks per year. These particular employees will normally work 8-hour shifts. So, therefore if you are going to be open for 5 days a week, and have decided that you need counselors to cover the center 8 hours a day for 1 year then you will have to budget for 3 FTE's as shown below.

$$40 \text{ hours} \times 52 \text{ weeks} = 2,080 \text{ total hours}$$
$$2,080 \times 3 \text{ employees} = 6,240 \text{ hours}$$
$$6,240/2,080 = 3 \text{ Full Time Equivalents (FTEs)}$$

A typical operating budget has several lines for position allocation. These lines are usually listed in a summary form by a dollar value. For example, the sum of $150,000 may be listed on a line entitled "Salaries." Accordingly, if you were to look at the detail of your budget by individual line item, it will be apparent that this money is allocated for 3 positions or 3 FTEs paid annually $50,000 each.

$$2{,}080 \text{ hours} / 52 \text{ weeks} = 40 \text{ hours per work week}$$
$$80 \text{ hours bi-weekly} \times \$24.03 = \$1{,}922.40$$
$$\$1{,}922.40 \times 26 \text{ bi-weekly pay periods} = \$49{,}982.40$$

Also, an important note to keep in mind when it comes to budgeting is that you will want to "round up" all figures on the budget line. Thus, for all intents and purposes, do not use cents and it is perfectly acceptable to round up. On top of employee salaries, this section of the budget should also include non-productive dollars and employee benefits. The final part of the budget is comprised of operating expenses such as supplies, professional fees, equipment rental, depreciation, utilities, and other operating expenses. Again, your goal should be to generate a budget that addresses each aspect of your business. One of the more common problems that organizations face are often unforeseen costs that are not accounted for during the initial budgeting process.

## Controls

The last section of the plan has to do with accountability. The process by which managers account for or direct the behavior of an organization is by using *Controls*. The controls that are deployed by management ensure that the goals of the company are being consistently achieved. These controls are set up at varying intervals and should be easily adapted to meet ongoing change within your operating environment. More to the point, many of the entities that you will seek funding from will also want to see the process by which you are going to oversee and regulate organizational progression and compliance. The following is an example of a fundable business plan.

# Global Health Care, Inc.
## Business Plan

### EXECUTIVE SUMMARY:

The 2005 Global Health Care, Inc., Business Plan for the renovation of our current New Jersey Licensed Ambulatory Health Care Facility seeks to increase revenue for the company. The gross sales target is $1,157,910 for the first year post-renovation. This goal seems to be attainable, given the increased need for community health care and preventative medicine.

### CURRENT MARKETING SITUATION:

The target area is located in Ward T, which consists of Summit and Mountain Top, Your County. The Census tracts are 55, 68, 72, 81, 11, 25, 58, and 26. Source of data is the Metropolitan Statistical Area Map, Any Town, NY. The patient base is African American (20%), Hispanics (8%), Caucasian (70%) and Asian (2%). This area is medically undeserved and located in a health profession shortage area.

### OPPORTUNITIES AND ISSUES ANALYSIS:

Considering that there are 450,000 women and children on welfare and Medicaid in New York, we are in an excellent position to deliver those vital medical services to those individuals and families in our area. Currently there are 54,200 people enrolled in Medicaid HMO's in Your County.

GLOBAL is licensed to provide medical, dental, vision, pharmacy and home health services. GLOBAL is currently providing pediatric services, which include immunizations, psychotherapy both individual and family, as well as substance abuse counseling and ancillary services. GLOBAL's current yearly encounter rate is 1,500. That is, we have provided 1,500 units of service so far this year, using just one exam room. We are now in an excellent position to expand our services and increase our patient encounters to 3,300.

Yet, in order to achieve this goal, GLOBAL must upgrade the existing facility to include, two exam rooms capable of providing pediatric, internal and OB/GYN medicine. Additionally, one dental exam room will be incorporated to service those low and moderate-income individuals and families that cannot or will not go to a dentist outside of their neighborhood.

One of the key factors that will contribute to GLOBAL's success is that the public is turning to community health care. The current philosophy is that hospitals have become known for being large, dark, cold and indifferent to patients. GLOBAL has built a strong reputation within the community for the last 10 years.

## OBJECTIVES:

GLOBAL's financial objectives for this business unit is as follows:

(1) Earn an annual rate of return on investment over the next year of 15%.

(2) Produce revenue of $1,157,910 within one year of completion of the renovation project.

(3) Achieve an encounter rate of 3,300 patients.

## MARKETING STRATEGY:

*Community Health Care Delivery Development and Testing*

### CONCEPT

What are the characteristics of the patients that utilize GLOBAL's services? What primary benefits will be built into these services? How can GLOBAL maintain its' patient flow?

Concept 1: Welfare/Medicaid Patients are generally prone to use hospital emergency rooms for treatment, in most cases, unnecessarily. Low and Moderate income earners as defined in US Census tract.

Concept 2: Essential medical and dental services that the community can use as an alternative to going to the hospital or not receiving any care at all. Patients will identify with health practitioners that reflect their values and community. As a result more accurate and complete medical histories can be obtained.

Concept 3: Presently, there are approximately 10 HMO's licensed to operate in Orange County or waiting approval. GLOBAL will be a part of all of these HMO's; HMO's pay providers a monthly capitation fee whether or not the patient comes in or not. The Physicians in GLOBAL's facility will be identified in the HMO network manuals. In addition, Foundation For All People, which is the agency working for the State of NY, to assist new and current enrollees with identifying physicians in their areas, will have GLOBAL's provider information available for those patients within the GLOBAL operating area.

## TESTING

Concept (3) Elaboration: All Welfare and Medicaid recipients in Orange County must choose an HMO before October 2005. Each HMO that is under state contract has to offer the same basic set of options including inpatient and outpatient services, primary and specialty care, family planning and prescription drugs. These services must be accessible to the community. This concept will be tested with a group of randomly selected residents.

Consumers are asked to respond to the following questions about the concept:

1. Are the benefits of community health care clear to you and believable? This measures the concept's *communicability* and *believability*. If the scores are low, the concept must be refined or revised.

2. Do you see these community services as solving a problem or filling a need for you? This measures the *need level*. Wherefore, the stronger the need for the service—the higher the expected consumer interest.

3. Do other service providers currently meet this need and satisfy you? This measures the *gap level* between the new services and existing services. Again, the greater the gap, the higher the expected consumer interest. The need level can be multiplied by the gap level to produce a *need-gap score*. The higher the need-gap score, the higher the expected interest. A high need-gap score means that the consumer views the service as filling a strong need *and* that he/she is not satisfied by available alternatives.

4. Are the prices reasonable in relationship to the value? This measures *perceived value*. The higher the perceived value, the higher the expected consumer interest.

5. Would you (definitely, probably, probably not, definitely not) use these community services? This measures *purchase intention*. We would expect it to be high for consumers who answered the previous three questions positively.

6. When and how often will the services be used? This provides an additional measure of service use and service frequency.

## PROMOTION

In order to come up with an effective promotional campaign we will address several issues beginning with motivational research. We will develop and test a hypothesis as to what our potential patients may be thinking about, when it comes to certain services. It is very important to note that a consumer uses a service with the future expectation that that particular service will yield a desired expectation and/or benefit. Health care delivery has become extremely sophisticated and complex. The emphasis is to contain costs while increasing the level of quality of service. Thus, we must identify our target consumers' decision-making processes as well as any cultural, social and personal beliefs and attitudes.

Furthermore, we can compliment our niche marketing with a *Service Innovation Strategy*. GLOBAL will be able to capitalize on the fact that we have provided services in the community without cost, in some instances, for the last seven years. The residents in the community have already experienced our dedication to providing services to those who were previously without the means to pay. Thus, we have developed a reputation for caring about our patients. This is especially important now that the state of New York has just introduced a health insurance plan for those low and moderate individuals that cannot afford health care. These patients are now in a position to utilize our services and pay for them.

## PRICING

### *GLOBAL Rate Per Encounter:

Individual Psychotherapy for Adults ..................................145
Individual Psychotherapy for Juveniles...............................175
Family Psychotherapy ......................................................130
Group Therapy ..................................................................55
Psychiatric Diagnosis and Evaluation ................................185
Psychiatric Counseling .....................................................150
Inpatient/Outpatient Referrals ..........................................170
Drug and Alcohol Screenings ...........................................170
Substance Abuse Outreach ................................................25
Pediatric Care Visits and Immunizations ..........................195
Urine Screenings (Drug and Alcohol)..................................87

### Medicaid/Welfare Rate Per Encounter:

Individual Psychotherapy for Adults ...................................36
Individual Psychotherapy for Juveniles ...............................46
Family Psychotherapy ....................................................42.50
Group Therapy ..................................................................30
Psychiatric Diagnosis and Evaluation .................................65
Psychiatric Counseling......................................................56
Inpatient/Outpatient Referrals...........................................52
Drug and Alcohol Screenings............................................62
Substance Abuse Outreach................................................30

Pediatric Care Visits and Immunizations.........................55
Urine Screenings (Drug and Alcohol)........................18.50

## Projected Patient Encounters for 2005:

Individual Psychotherapy for Adults ...............................600
Individual Psychotherapy for Juveniles ...........................200
Family Psychotherapy ...............................................100
Group Therapy ......................................................400
Psychiatric Diagnosis and Evaluation ..............................500
Psychiatric Counseling..............................................300
Inpatient/Outpatient Referrals......................................550
Drug and Alcohol Screenings........................................300
Substance Abuse Outreach..........................................200
Pediatric Care Visits and Immunizations ...........................200
Urine Screenings (Drug and Alcohol)..............................1000

GLOBAL projects that it will have approximately 3,300 patient encounters during fiscal 2005. The total costs to deliver these services, based upon this projection, would be $1,151,803 in year one. The median income limit for an Any City family for FY 2004 is $49,500.00. Additionally, those individuals and families without major insurance will be put on a sliding fee scale.

Moreover, by using a <u>community based health care facility</u> such as GLOBAL, the savings to the community would be quite substantial. For example, many of the residents of Any City who are low and moderate income earners generally go to the hospital emergency room for all types of treatment, including drug and alcohol related health problems. One ER visit costs about $30,000. If the hospital were to handle 750 of these encounters, it would cost $22,500,000 a year. If GLOBAL were to treat those same patients, it would cost *only* $1,151,803. Thus, Any City would save over $21 million dollars.

Furthermore, if those individuals who are seeking Inpatient/Outpatient Referrals and Drug/Alcohol Screenings were to come to GLOBAL as opposed to going to the Any City Hospital, or other hospitals in the area, the savings to the public would be an additional $260,000.00. In addition to the savings, GLOBAL would be in a perfect position to track those individuals and help the City contain future medical, as well as those social costs associated with drug abuse, such as AIDS and homelessness. Again, GLOBAL is a New York licensed ambulatory health care facility, specializing in outpatient substance abuse.

## BUDGET

*Global Health Care, Inc.*
*Clinic Project*

| | |
|---|---|
| Leasehold Improvements | $100,000 |
| Equipment | $55,000 |
| Operations | $550,000 |
| Marketing | $60,000 |

TOTAL ................................................................................... $765,000

Total Capital in Place: .......................................................... $3,500
Difference: ............................................................................. $761,500

Global Health Care, Inc.
Operating Budget Summary
January 1, 2005 - December 31, 2006

Administration Salaries: ..................................................... $380,220
Fringe - 15% ........................................................................ $57,033
Total Salaries & Fringes: .................................................... $437,253
Consultants: ......................................................................... $25,000
Space Cost: ........................................................................... $20,000
Travel: .................................................................................. $1,550
Consumable Supplies: .......................................................... $3,000
Equipment: ........................................................................... $55,000
Other Costs: ......................................................................... $610,000

Total Budget ........................................................................ $1,151,803

## Revenues

| Source: | Amount: |
| --- | --- |
| City of Goodwill | $456,010 |
| Third Party Billing | $576,900 |
| Fundraising | $90,000 |
| Donations | $35,000 |
| Total Revenues: | $1,157,910 |

## Controls

Management will determine whether or not goals are being met by reviewing those goals and the budget each quarter. Management will monitor promotion mix and the marketing strategy for adjustments and weaknesses. Should changes be necessary, management will refer back to the marketing strategy and methodically to go over the plan until material weaknesses have been discovered and adequate adjustments have been made accordingly.

# Chapter 7
# Revenue

The revenue section is perhaps the most important segment of this book. Revenue is the life's blood of the organization, and without a steady flow of it, the company will not survive. An organization must be able to generate a positive cash flow at all times during the year. Cash flow must be constant, and consistent, and it has to come in daily. Why daily? Well let's start by defining your revenue. Revenue has many different forms. It can be cash that is generated by the organization as a result of providing specific services. Revenue may also come from grants, donations and fundraisers. It is very important to note that there are two distinct types of money.

## Unrestricted Money

The first category is restricted and the second is unrestricted. Most people are familiar with unrestricted money. This money does not have any specific requirements from the funding source except to spend the money in support of the organization's mission. These types of funds are generally received in the form of donations and fundraisers. However, you must take into consideration that your local government may have explicit policies on the methods that can be used to raise these funds. It is a good practice to be consistent when it comes to fundraisers. The ideal fundraiser is held the same time each year. And also make certain that the public is presented with the outcome of the previous year. It is imperative and vital that your donors are made aware of the success that was achieved by their previous philanthropy and kindness. In effect, this type of consistent updating puts you in a position where you can have a fundraiser at anytime of the year. The timing of these events will depend solely on the goals outlined within your business plan. The best way to make sure that your events are a success is to form a fundraising committee with a board member serving as the chairperson. Again, this is another reason to pick your board members wisely. And, rest assured there are many people in your area that you know who will be honored to participate in these worthy endeavors.

## Restricted Money

Restricted funds are just that—restricted. These funds are designed for a certain purpose, and must be used for that purpose. No exceptions. This cash comes in the form of grants, endowments, bequests, legacies and awards. It should be designated restricted up front. And, for various reasons there can be many limitations on these funds. There are some grants that have to be spent within a certain amount of time. If the money is not used within the allocated time period it may have to be returned. Additionally, there are many legal rules and stipulations that must be adhered to without fail. For instance, the endowment that you received money from has clearly stated that all money must be utilized to purchase computers for the organization's business office. The bottom line is that computers must be brought, and used for that particular office. Yet, you may find provisions that state that the configuration of the hardware may be altered, just as long as the total amount of cash that was designated is accounted for in full. Another place where fund restrictions are found is on the salary line of the budget. This is a major area of contention and a primary focus of grants administrators and auditors.

## Commingling Funds

Many organizations run into trouble when it comes to following the agreed upon allocation of restricted money. This is not to say that these organizations are not trust worthy, but, too often if their cash flow is not consistent they may divert funds to other immediate areas that are experiencing shortfalls. This is the lethal process of commingling funds. The finance section outlines this topic in detail, however, it is important to note that this type of accounting is wholly unacceptable, and produces unwanted financial and perhaps legal consequences. There are many great opportunities to obtain very large amounts of these restricted and unrestricted funds and getting this money is a good thing. It is just quintessential that you start from the beginning to use it in the correct way. Equally, this money is not to be shunned away from or turned down. In due course, all that is necessary is that you keep clean books, follow the rules and manage your organization with business acumen. It is just that simple.

The cash that comes into the company as a direct result of the organization providing service is unrestricted money. This is money that comes in the form of client and patient payments, insurance company remittances and other third party arrangements. According to your business plan this money can be used for whatever expenses that you have previously identified. This money can be moved from one budget line to another without consequence. For example, your volume is up, and you need to hire another counselor, yet, the salary line on the budget is exhausted—what can you do? Well, if there is $50,000 in unrestricted money sitting on the equipment line that has not been used you can simply reallocate that money to the salary line and hire the new employee. Just keep in mind that the purchase of that equipment may be delayed until the cash comes in from the extra volume.

## Medical Doctors

The revenue sources that can be generated should include a diverse mix of fee-for-service, managed care, capitation payments and in some organizations clinical trials. Yet again, daily cash flow is a sign of good health. In order to get a good idea of which source of revenue that you should concentrate on let's take a look at the industry as it relates to fee-for-service vs. managed care contracting. This section will be of particular importance to medical doctors, and if you plan to include primary care within your organization. Primary care is essential to the practice of behavioral healthcare in that many patients are comorbid. The topic of comorbidity is discussed in greater detail in the section regarding the organization's Primary Care and Pharmacotherapy Program operating structure.

Current healthcare reform has taken on a dynamic life of it's own, it has many complicated payment structures and it is extremely necessary for you to understand the payment principals within this environment. The present reimbursement environment is a mix of fee-for-service and managed care. In this new environment of managed care organizations (MCOs) healthcare providers are going out of business at an alarming pace. Many self-employed physicians that have been in practice for years are finding that they cannot survive in this new market without making some serious organizational adjustments. In the past, patients that normally went to a physicians' office would come in and either pay for services rendered, or present an insurance plan. The practice had the option of either accepting the insurance, or asking the patient to pay up front, and subsequently the patient would send in their own claim forms to their managed care organization (MCO) for payment.

# Physicians Understand

Many physicians understood that managed care would come along one day; however, there was no way of knowing that the influence that they wield today is beyond belief. MCOs have literally taken over the healthcare market place. However, there are still some fee-for-service plans, yet, very few remain. It is a fact that many doctors saw their practices slowly fading away; nonetheless, many of them could not explain or even understand this complex issue until they were at critical mass. Hence, when an MCO comes into a particular market its' mission is to recruit as many new members to their panel as possible. This is done geographically. On the other hand, if a particular doctor, or office is not willing to participate with that MCO then all of those patients that normally would have come to that office can no longer do so. If they chose to remain with that provider then the visit or service is considered to be out of network. A couple of monetary things could happen at that point, either the provider asks for the cash before the visit or he/she could wait for a reduced payment from the patient's out of network benefit provision. The decision has to be made with your cash flow in mind. If you have a strong cash flow, then the delay and reduced payment may be considered. However, if your cash flow is slow then you will want to take the payment ahead of the appointment. The downside is that you are definitely going to have attrition and a drop in volume.

## Closing Enrollment

Overnight some practices went from 1,000 patients to just 400. Once the practice looses those patients usually they will not see them again. The time when a doctor could just hang his/her shingle on the door and a multitude of patients would just come into their business—has ended. Now one has to go out and actively market to recruit patients. Unfortunately, many doctors are good doctors and not good businessman. And, thus lack the business acumen and marketing skills necessary to compete and take clear leadership positions within their various markets.

Furthermore, to limit costs MCOs are now aggressively deciding which doctors can actually participate in their healthcare networks. This can be devastating for a practice if the MCO states that they are closing enrollment. A doctor that is not a participant in an MCO that has a major share of the patient population in his/her area will certainly be in jeopardy of not having enough patients to sustain the practice. Moreover, many MCOs pay a set capitation fee monthly for each patient that is assigned to a physician. This fee can be extremely low. For example, a doctor may receive $17.00 monthly to treat a member of an MCO. In a traditional fee-for-service environment that doctor could have billed the patient $100-$300 for each visit. As a result, not only is the practice going to learn to survive with more competition for patients, they're going to have to allow for reduced revenue as well. Nevertheless, if you are in the network, the way around this is to have as many patients signed up for your organization as possible. The fact of the matter is that statistically many patients come into the office very infrequently. Yet, the monthly payment will be made to your organization no matter how many times the patient actually comes into the facility. And, the additional benefit is that the insurance company will respect your organizations' strength because of the substantial number of members that are assigned to your providers.

# Chapter 8
# Grants

A grant award is a significant source of revenue for your organization. And also, there are no limits as to how many of these grants that you can receive. These grants are strictly needs based and are awarded to the organization that can identify and service a specific lack of something essential in the community. For the most part grants are historical in nature and set up with particular goals in mind. And, whoever submits a proposal that appears to fully address the issues outlined in the grantors request will get an award. Plus, you'll also discover that the variety of grants is endless. There are grants to purchase land, construction, program creation and development, food services, medicine, medical supplies and the list goes on. There are a number of sources for these funds including your local town, state and Federal government. However, the funding authority does require the necessary structure that was outlined in the corporate section to be in place prior to any award.

## Community Development Block Grants (CDBG)

The funding that comes from the Federal government normally passes through your town in the form of Community Development Block Grants (CDBG). Theses grants are renewable on an annual basis and are usually not automatically renewed. Yet, many of the non-profits that do eventually receive these funds continue to do so for many years. In some of the larger cities there are millions of dollars available for distribution on an annual basis. How do you apply for this money? An application can be picked up at your towns' grant administration office usually during business hours. It is vital that you make a positive contact within that office. The reason is that this office decides which completed applications for funding make it to the local council for approval. In other words, this office assesses and analyzes all applications in detail for compliance to published submission requirements, and program applicability.

This administrative office is a part of your local government and has the responsibility to monitor and administer most grants. The Federal Department of Housing and Urban Development, which oversees these grants, allow local governments to administer, evaluate and to distribute these funds based upon local standards. For the most part, the major drivers of these awards lie in the amounts of people that the program intends to service during their budget year. Thus, a significant amount of weight is put on the applications that service large populations, and who can subsequently predict future rises in current service levels. In addition, the application will also seek information pertaining to prior year levels of service delivery. Historically, the most successful organizations that ultimately receive funding are proactive in this process. The rule of "Politics 101" is to make sure that you have an advocate vigorously working to present your case for funding all year round. Once more, it is of the utmost importance that your organization has board members that are active in the community at the highest governmental levels possible.

The grants administration office has many different operational and financial responsibilities such as program compliance reviews and audits. Thus, at any time a representative from this office can come to your site and visually monitor program activities. In fact, it is not unusual if someone does come out to review your program at scheduled and unscheduled intervals during the award period. During the visit the auditor can ask to view your financial records in relationship to the grant. This is another reason to make sure that your books are always in order and are clearly transparent. Normally, if there are not any overt concerns with your program the inspections are superficial and cordial. However, if there are issues and concerns with the way you are spending public monies, then make sure that you are prepared to elaborate in detail exactly how you are deploying those allocated resources.

## Technical Assistance

On the other hand, in an effort to assist grantees, many of these offices have full time personnel who are available to support new and established organizations with the development of their programs, and to provide technical assistance. The technical assistance part is crucial, as many of the requirements to receive funding can be explained to you in detail and any impending issues can be worked out with the aid of these technicians. In fact, this assistance is so instrumental that the Federal government requires these administrators to provide this assistance to you at no charge, and to staff these offices accordingly. As a matter of fact, within the larger towns that administer hefty grant awards you'll find a variety of people that specialize in precise areas such as budgeting, operations and personnel.

In view of this fact, these folks are there for support and assistance only; they are not there to run your business. It is your responsibility to learn and to put together a competent team of managers to perpetuate your organization. What is more, listed in the grants administration office you should find applications and timetables for other current grants and funding opportunities.

## Positive Revenue Management

In general, the grant process flows in this manner (1) submission of a completed grant application, (2) grants administration review, (3) public comment, (4) local government approval, and (5) upon approval and commencement of the grant cycle an organization can now submit vouchers to draw down on their funds in predetermined increments. As the leader of your organization it is of the essence that you attend all public and allowable private discussions concerning your funding. Many states have implemented "Sunshine Acts" which specify that the public should have the right to be present to witness deliberations, decision-making and policy formulations within their local governments. The upside to this calculated and sensible routine is that you will be able to minimize any surprises, or be there in case of any questions, or should concerns arise in relationship to your program. This is the process of positive revenue management. Whereas, you learn to consistently follow your revenue stream within your ecosystem. If there is an impending logjam, you may be able to clear it up immediately without a negative revenue impact to the program.

## State Grant Funding

During the year your state also receives grant funding from the state government to administer to local non-profits. On top of that, your state government also sets aside funding within its own budget that is intended to be distributed to non-profits in the form of state funded grants. These grants can range in variety from AIDS to Victims of Alzheimer's disease. The Federal government, state and other sources of revenue, fund many of these grants jointly. The source of funding dictates the grant period, grant amount and the type of requirements necessary to apply and successfully win an award.

The categories are generally broken down into components such as direct service to a population, research in an identified field, surveillance, education, outreach, prevention, and housing services. The public will normally be notified of an impending grant by way of the Internet, news media, and directly through a specific department within your state such as the Department of Health and Senior Services. The Department of Health is the primary entity that will fund counseling and behavioral healthcare. The notice of grant availability (Fig. 7-1) normally is published with all of the specific information necessary to decide whether, or not, you are interested in pursuing a certain grant, and if your organization will meet the published funding requirements.

# NOTICE OF GRANT AVAILABILITY

**NAME OF GRANT PROGRAM:**
Treatment for individuals with HIV and their Families.

**STATUTORY AUTHORITY:**     **GRANT PROGRAM NO. 05-11-AIDS**
Kentucky Statute 26:5             **TYPE OF AWARDS TO BE ISSUED:**
C-1 et seq.                           Cost-reimbursement Grants
                                            and/or Letters of Agreement

**PURPOSE FOR WHICH THE GRANT PROGRAM FUNDS WILL BE USED:**
To develop a coordinated continuum of care for individuals with HIV and their families. Specific activities include medical and nursing care, dental, outreach, drug treatment services, case management, housing and support services.

**AMOUNT OF MONEY IN THE GRANT PROGRAM:**
Grants range from $25,000 to $1,500,000. Awards begin on July 1, 2004 and will be made for a 12-month budget period. Funding estimates may vary and are subject to the Annual Appropriation Act. Continuation awards will be made based on satisfactory progress and evaluation, and availability of funds. Current recipients of health service grants who have performed satisfactorily will be given first priority for continued funding.

**ELIGIBLE APPLICANTS MUST COMPLY WITH THE FOLLOWING REQUIREMENTS:**
1. Terms and Conditions for the Administration of Grants.
2. General and specific Grant Compliance requirements issued by the Granting Agency.
3. Applicable Federal Cost Principles relating to the Applicant.

**GROUP OR ENTITIES WHICH MAY APPLY FOR THE GRANT PROGRAM:**
Local government agencies, state agencies, private non-profit corporations, hospitals, local health departments, municipalities, and community-based agencies. Preference will be given to current recipients of grants.

**QUALIFICATIONS NEEDED BY APPLICANT TO BE CONSIDERED FOR A GRANT:**
Experience with the provision of community health and social services. Experience with HIV/AIDS and/or affected populations. Appropriate professional licenses and compliance with appropriate regulations.

**APPLICATION PROCEDURES:**
Submit a 1-2 page concept paper to contact below delineating goals and objectives, and a brief budget. Based on the availability of funds, a Request for Application (RFA) will be released to eligible entities, including those who have submitted concept papers.

**FOR INFORMATION CONTACT:**
Director, Care and Treatment Unit
Division of HIV/AIDS Services TELEPHONE: (123) 456-7890

*Matt Hamilton, MBA, Ph.D.*

P.O. Box 123 FAX: (123) 456-789
Trenton, KY 08625-0363 E-MAIL: yourcontact@doh.state.ky.us

**DEADLINE BY WHICH APPLICATIONS MUST BE SUBMITTED:**
Varies by grant. Information will be included in the Request for Application. Concept papers will be accepted throughout the year.

**DATE BY WHICH APPLICANT SHALL BE NOTIFIED WHETHER THEY WILL RECEIVE FUNDS:**
Applicant will be notified within one month of the beginning of the project period.

**FIGURE 7-1.** Grant availability notice.

To obtain further details regarding a certain grant you must ask for a Request for Application (RFA). The RFA will have all applicable deadlines, submission and compliance requirements. Normally, the grant application will have a cover sheet see figure 7-2.

## GRANT APPLICATION PACKAGE COVERSHEET

1. Instructions for Completion of "Application for Grant Funds."
2. Application for Grant Funds
3. Statement of Local Health Officer
4. Needs and Objectives
5. Method(s) and Evaluation of Project
6. Cost Summary
7. Funds and Program Income from Other Sources
8. Schedule A – Board of Directors List
9. Schedule B – Certification Regarding Debarment and Suspension
10. Schedule C – Agency Minority Profile
11. Schedule D – Certification Sheet
12. Schedule E – Other Cost Categories
13. Schedule F – Personnel Cost
14. Schedule G – Personnel Justification
15. Schedule H – Consultant Services Costs
16. Schedule I – Consultant Services Justification
17. Schedule J – Other Cost Justification
18. Schedule K – Certification Regarding Lobbying
19. Schedule L – Certified Audit
20. Multi-Year Grant Budget Request (Form 15) and Instructions - to be completed only for 1st and 2nd multi-year grant.

**FIGURE 7-2**. Grant application cover sheet.

This guide is a specific list of information that is generally requested by most funding sources. So again, it would be prudent to put together a standard package where all of this information can be found in a timely manner. Whereas, there are going to be some occasions that you will learn about a grant at the last minute. In some instances the deadline to turn in your RFP may be just hours away.

Surely, there is not going to be any time to waste looking for the required documents. The rules for submission are often very explicit and strict.

Simply put, if your application is not complete you may not get a second chance for corrections. This can happen even if there is only one document missing from your package. Therefore, pay careful attention to the proposed coversheet. A good idea is to let someone who was not involved in the preparation of the grant go over the checklist for you. A fresh pair of eyes almost always increases your chances to submit a complete application on time.

## Hiring Grant Writers

Every organization should have at least one competent grant writer available to work on RFP's. Grant writing is a skill that is learned by doing. The best grant writer is a person that has a good sense of vision. This person must be able to submit a proposal that makes sense, and has unequivocally portrayed your organization's ability to deliver a particular service to a group of experienced reviewers. There are many people who may portray themselves as grant writers, but be aware.

A proven writer will be able to provide you with references of agencies that have actually received money from an accepted grant proposal that was submitted by this person. There is a big difference between submitting a grant, and winning an award. Many would-be grant writers will be quick to tell you that they have submitted a high volume of grants. However, there was always a problem that had to do with the organization itself. Some of this may be so; nevertheless, not everyone out there is shooting themselves in the foot. Once, an agency has found a good writer, they rarely like to share this contact with others for obvious reasons.

## Ongoing Submission

An agency with a multi-million dollar budget will normally have a salaried writer on staff. This person is generally responsible for the ongoing submission of applicable grant proposals. Most of their time is spent attending mandatory conferences and doing research in relation to upcoming RFP's. This is an extremely difficult position to fill as the work is very detailed and the proposal itself has to be free of errors in both the service delivery section and the budget. Oftentimes, the writer will request help from the accounting department for input on the budget and to ask for organizational cost information. There are normally three cost principles depending on the type of organization receiving grant funds (1) State and Local Governments, (2) Educational Institutions and (3) Not-for-Profit Organizations. The purpose of these principles is to determine and to outline the costs that are applicable to specific grants. Additionally, these principals are designed to ensure that your organization is allocating these costs according to generally accepted accounting principals (GAAP). Most grant writers are familiar with these costs and will write them into the grant accordingly. For instance, some funding sources do not allow management costs to be taken out of grant funds.

## Tight Niche Group

What if you do not have the money to hire a full time writer? There are some writers that will work on a project-by-project basis. The average grants writer is a person that is dedicated to working with non-profits; so many of them are aware that there are companies who cannot readily pay huge sums of money upfront. As a result, many will write up contracts that specify installment payments. It is advisable that this arrangement be based upon a realistic payment schedule that can be met in a timely manner. The bottom line here is that grant writers are a tight niche group, and they usually know each other. It would not be long until your organization gets "black listed" for non-payment. This situation can lead to a steep loss in revenue for your program. Ideally, you are going to want to submit many grant applications that have the potential of bringing in hundreds of thousands of dollars. So as a matter of sound management—pay your grant writer on time. Unfortunately, there are going to be times that you are not going to receive an award, even after paying out the money for the writer. Nonetheless, this is a part of doing business that you should anticipate, and take into consideration.

## Experiential Reservoir

How much should it cost? These costs can vary widely and may range anywhere from a low of $200 to $7,000 or more for a completed proposal. The factors that go into the calculation of charges are normally based upon the size, complexity of the grant and the grant writers' business structure. In that, independent writers will invariably charge less than grant writing companies as a whole. A good example would be that of a Ph.D., who offers independent grant consulting services including technical reviews. This would be the ideal situation, as many of the more business-like companies will have these doctors on staff. Therefore, your organization will receive the same professional skill level usually found in a research oriented Ph.D., but, without paying for the overhead. In fact, the individual writer will have a bit more flexibility in terms of schedule and financial matters. Yet, there are benefits of having a group do your grant writing. Whereas, within a sizeable group of academics you are certainly going to find a larger experiential reservoir of program knowledge. No matter which direction that you choose, always verify references. Perhaps, the best source of information regarding a candidate would come from the funding source directly, if available.

The following sample grant proposal was designed to obtain funding for a new construction project that includes medical equipment and office furniture. This particular proposal is setup to support the creation of an integrated healthcare delivery system that includes pharmacotherapy.

## *Grant Proposal Example*

### Hamilton Health Care, Inc.

### Section A

### Development Plan Summary

1) *The proposal*:

To utilize public grant monies to construct an ambulatory care drug counseling & case management facility. The new facility will be a Community Based Comprehensive Primary Care Health Center.

2003 Grant Awards and others:

a) City of Any City - CDBG ................................................$200,000
b) County of Goodwill ......................................................$300,000
c) Mortgage - Bank ..........................................................$308,961

2) *The project*:

Community Based Comprehensive Health Care Center

123 (Sunny Lane Section)

Blue Ridge, Any Town USA

Description: 8000 sq. ft. Comprehensive Primary Care Facility providing high quality health care and continuity of care to local residents.

3)   *The Owner/Developer/Manager*:

Hamilton Health Care, Inc.

456 Pleasant Way

Hilltop, Any City USA

An Illinois State Department of Health Licensed Primary Care Provider. Developer/ Manager of a small (5000 sq. ft.) community based primary care center at XYZ Lane.

4)   *Description of project*:

Construction will consist of the demolition of existing structure, site excavation and the new construction of an estimated 8000 sq. ft., facility with 6500 sq. ft. program usable space.

5)   *Comprehensive Community Based Health Center*:

Hamilton Health Care Inc., will build on its existing capacity by the expansion into comprehensive primary care. This will provide the community with a sound infrastructure in a system of care that is capable of responding to community needs.

6)   *Preliminary estimated project costs*:

| | |
|---|---|
| Construction cost | $487,960 |
| Equipment | $64,000 |
| Furniture | $40,000 |
| Soft costs | $217,001 |
| Total project cost: | $808,961 |

7) *Source of development funds*:

a) City of Any City - CDBG ...............................................$200,000

b) County of Goodwill .......................................................$300,000

c) Mortgage - Bank ...........................................................$308,961

8) *Productivity*: (6 months)

a) XYZ Lane - 4000 sq. ft.

Monthly gross receipt - $650,000

Client encounters - 8,780

b) 123 (Sunny Lane Section) - 8000 sq. ft.

Project annual gross - $10,000,000

Projected annual encounters - 10,000

Development Plan Strategy

Strategic Planning

Hamilton Health Care, Inc., has grown from an ambulatory case management, counseling and referral organization into a primary care provider. This metamorphosis came about as the result of an unmet community need left vacant by the local health care system. The health care needs in the Sunnyview section of Colonia are overwhelming. In order to implement immediate and long-term planning and operational procedures, HAMILTON proposes as part of the overall development strategy to implement a Technical Operating Plan for the community based health care center.

Technical Operating Plan:

The plan will focus primarily on the community-based center's essential components such as:

- Community needs
- Center's - mission, goals, objectives
- Governance
- Management/ Administration
- Clinical program

Section B

Development Plan

*Proposal*

Hamilton Health Care, Inc., (HAMILTON) is requesting assistance to acquire and develop a city owned site at 123 Sunny Lane Section Blue Ridge, Anytown USA. The site will be developed into a new Community Based Health Care Center. The Community Based Health Care Center will be a Comprehensive Primary Care Center located in a neighborhood with a multitude of health problems and illnesses. In 2003, HAMILTON was granted site control of 123 Sunny Lane Section, to construct a new ambulatory care counseling facility. The City of AnyCity awarded $500,000 Community Development Block Grant (CDBG) funds for development. Also the State of Goodwill awarded $650,000 to develop the facility.

Since receiving the above grant awards the HAMILTON operation has changed from a purely counseling case management operation to a community primary care provider. After years of providing counseling and referrals, in 2004 HAMILTON became a Licensed Primary Care Provider by the Illinois State Department of Health. The licensing of HAMILTON as a primary care provider brought the organization to a higher operating level as a supplier of health care services. However, as a community primary care provider HAMILTON realizes that its current facility of 4000 sq. ft. cannot meet the overwhelming needs of the community. The current center at XYZ Lane will become an SBU satellite facility to the primary care service center to be built at 123 Sunny Lane Section. Therefore, HAMILTON is requesting that the two previous grants from the City and State be mobilized as development and hard cost monies to start the development process to construct a new community based comprehensive primary care health center.

Developer - Owner – Operator

Hamilton Health Care, Inc., is a non-profit community based organization founded in 2002, with a mandate to provide counseling, medical and social services to women, adolescents and families who are "AT RISK" in the community. HAMILTON a young organization less than 10 years old has been very active in providing health care assistance to the undeserved, the poor and the at risk populations of the distressed neighborhoods of Goodwill.

Still, after several years of providing case management and referral services; HAMILTON realized the need to become more clinical in its delivery of health care services. In an effort to meet the challenges facing its clients, HAMILTON became a licensed Primary Care Provider by the Illinois Department of Health. In December 2003, HAMILTON opened a newly renovated 4000 sq. ft. Primary Care Facility at XYZ Lane. The operation of this facility over the next four years will give HAMILTON many of the essentials needed to operate the more all-inclusive primary care center. Given, the overwhelming need for a comprehensive community based health care delivery system HAMILTON is in a very good position to lead the way in meeting this need.

Integrated System of Care

The newly constructed Comprehensive Health Center at 123 Sunny Lane Section will provide a system of care consisting of the following:
- Primary Care Services
- Diagnostic Laboratory
- X-Ray - Radiology Services
- Pharmacy
- Alternative Care Services
- Translation Services
- Preventive Health - Dental Services
- Essential Supplementary, Supportive and Environment Services

The Center's Clinical Program will be designed to facilitate the following critical elements of patient care:

- High Quality Services
- Continuity of Care
- Hospitalization
- Availability
- Accessibility
- Comprehensiveness
- Coordination
- Clinical Teams
- Integration - Local Health Care System

A mixture of services will be delivered to meet the needs of the community. Moreover, HAMILTON in the strategic planning for the center will prioritize the community needs to ensure a continuity of care through the Local Health Care System.

## *Detail of Productivity*

A.    XYZ Lane

Since opening in December 2002, this facility is operating around 90% of capacity generating revenue of $650,000 a month. Monthly encounters are hovering around 1000. This center is expected to peak over gross revenue of $1,000,000 and average monthly encounters of 1200.

B. Comprehensive Health Center - 123 Sunny Lane Section

Anticipated opening: November 2004.

1st year Revenue - $10,000,000

1st year Service Level - 22,000

## CURRENT NEEDS ASSESSMENT

The health care needs in the City of Any City are overwhelming the community. The poor neighborhoods and "at risk" populations are suffering from a multitude of illnesses. Currently, the City's existing facilities for treatment and education cannot meet the large and growing demand for health care services. Moreover, the paradigm shifts of recent years have increased the need for more comprehensive community based health care delivery systems. Hamilton's growth from a case management referral organization into primary care provider has brought the organization closer to meeting the needs of the community. In order to approach the massive task of high quality health care delivery, HAMILTON will focus on prioritizing the problems as a base for strategic planning. A formal needs assessment of the service area, which will identify the resources and clinical capabilities required to establish and sustain the proposed community-based health facility has been conducted. Subsequently, our development plan strategy is to implement a technical operating plan for the proposed center.

*Technical Operating Plan*

Formulate a management, clinical and operational approach for the proposed comprehensive health center to ensure the provision of high quality health care and continuity of care within the local system. We have developed an ongoing long-term planning and operational approach to perpetuate the following:

a.) Broadening HAMILTON's existing capacity by building upon the organization's Primary Care Center at XYZ Lane.

b.) The design of a new larger facility to maximize operational efficiency and service delivery.

c.) Assessment of the types of services best suited for the target population, center's clinical program and available resources.

d.) Implementation of procedures and systems for management, clinical, governance and operation of the center.

As part of HAMILTON's development plan, a Technical Operating Task plan will be structured as a guide for the technical operating plan's development and implementation.

## *Development Schedule*

Project: Community Based Health Center
123 Sunnyview Way
Anytown, USA

| Date | Task |
| --- | --- |
| 1. November 2003 | Formation – Dev. Team |
| 2. November - December 16 | Planning – Fin. Structuring |
| 3. January - March 2004 | Architect Designs |
| 4. January - March 2004 | Financial Packaging |
| 5. January - March 2004 | Technical Operating Plan |
| 6. May 2004 | Architect Planning Board |

| | |
|---|---|
| 7. June 2004 | Cost Estimates |
| 8. June 2004 | Financial GAP financing |
| 9. July 2004 | Working Drawing |
| 10. August 2004 | Bidding |
| 11. September 2004 | Selection of Contractor |
| 12. September 2004 | Closing - GAP financing |
| 13. October 2004 | Construction Start |
| 14. January 2005 | Construction Completion |
| 15. March 2005 | Grand Opening |

*Matt Hamilton, MBA, Ph.D.*

## Hamilton Health Care Inc.
*Project Budget 2004*

Community Based Health Care Center
123 Sunny Lane Section
Anytown, USA

## Construction Project Budget
8000 sq. ft. of building gross floor costs.

| Items | Quantity | Unit | Total |
|---|---|---|---|
| General Conditions | 1 | $46,000 | $46,000 |
| Demolition of Building | 1 | $24,000 | $24,000 |
| Site Preparation | 1 | $5,000 | $5,000 |
| Earthwork | 1 | $17,000 | $17,000 |
| Paving and Surfacing | 1 | $18,100 | $18,100 |
| Site Utilities | 1 | $16,000 | $16,000 |
| Site Improvements | 1 | $12,000 | $12,000 |
| Landscaping | 1 | $4,000 | $4,000 |
| Cast-in-place concrete | 1 | $23,000 | $23,000 |
| Unit masonry | 1 | $46,000 | $46,000 |
| Rough Carpentry | 1 | $18,000 | $18,000 |
| Finish Carpentry | 1 | $16,000 | $16,000 |
| Waterproofing | 1 | $1,500 | $1,500 |
| Roof and sheet metal | 1 | $21,600 | $21,600 |
| Joint Sealers | 1 | $1,500 | $1,500 |
| Doors and Frames | 1 | $12,000 | $12,000 |

| | | | |
|---|---|---|---|
| Metal Windows | 1 | $10,000 | $10,000 |
| Finish Hardware | 1 | $6,500 | $6,500 |
| Glazing | 1 | $1,500 | $1,500 |
| Gypsum Wall Board | 1 | $18,000 | $18,000 |
| Acoustical Ceiling | 1 | $10,700 | $10,700 |
| Resilient Flooring | 2 | $6,400 | $12,800 |
| Painting | 1 | $7,000 | $7,000 |
| Toilet Accessories | 1 | $2,000 | $2,000 |
| Plumbing | 1 | $16,000 | $16,000 |
| HVAC | 1 | $40,000 | $40,000 |
| Electrical | 1 | $56,000 | $56,000 |
| | | *Subtotal*: | $443,360 |
| Contingency (10%) | | | $44,360 |
| Total Floor Costs Budget | | | $487,960 |
| Equipment | | | $64,000 |
| Furniture | | | $40,000 |
| | | *Total Construction Budget*: | $591,960 |

## HAMILTON - CBHCC

*Development Budget*

Soft Costs:

| | |
|---|---|
| Architect/Engineer | $48,000 |
| Acquisition | $1 |
| Consultant fees | $30,000 |
| Bank fees | $26,000 |
| Legal fees - owner | $6,000 |
| Insurance - Builders risk | $6,000 |
| Technical operating plan | $15,000 |
| Survey - Environmental | $3,500 |
| Carry costs | $6,000 |
| Accounting/audit | $6,000 |
| Fees/permits | $3,000 |
| Printing | $1,500 |
| Construction Interest | $21,000 |
| Project contingency | $15,000 |
| Developers fee | $30,000 |
| *Total Development costs:* | $<u>217,001</u> |
| *Total Project Costs:* | $**<u>808,961</u>** |

*Proposed Sources for Development Funds*

1) City of Any City - CDBG ................................................. $200,000
2) County of Goodwill ........................................................ $300,000
3) Mortgage - Bank ............................................................ $308,961
                             *Totals*: ................................. $<u>808,961</u>

# Chapter 9
# Loans

Low interest loans are an important part of your overall financial portfolio. The different types of loans that you can take out are Small Business Loans (SBA), commercial bank business loans, personal loans, credit union loans, economic development loans, special segment loans, real estate equity loans, leasing and equipment financing, overdraft accounts, lines of credit, friends and family and term loans. These loans can be structured to match your borrowing needs, or to match the life of the financed asset. In addition, repayment can be tailored to fit your cash flow and many of these loans can be unsecured or secured, with flexible collateral options. Yet, most importantly the banks offer fixed or floating rates that are available depending on market conditions.

## Economic Development

As you can see there are many outlets in which you can raise capital for your organization. And, amazingly one particular loan source that is derived from individual state casino tax collections is relatively unknown to most small businesses. In fact, this particular loan does not require a great deal of paperwork and has a very low interest rate. Hence, for this reason, and the fast turnaround time, it is a very attractive loan source. And, it comes directly through your state's department of economic development. Why economic development? The economic development department is designed to assist the state in the creation of jobs and to grow and sustain economic development. Therefore, if your organization has a project that encourages job growth, and community development then you have a good chance for a loan. However, the money that is available for investment is limited, and is replenished yearly. So, if you are interested in applying for this money call you state office of economic development for more information. Usually, this department will assign you a loan officer that has a great deal of experience in your particular business who will work with you to review, and organize your business plan. The economic development department is a great source of expertise.

## Leverage Cash

The ultimate decision on which type of loan that you will apply for will depend on your goals as defined in the business plan. The ideal loan that can be immediately put into effect with little paperwork is the overdraft feature on your business checking account. The bank that you chose to open your business account should be where you have a personal relationship with the branch manager. The branch manger can assist you with the necessary paperwork to add this feature to your business account that perhaps is in place on your personal account. The idea is to be able to leverage cash in the event that you experience a brief interruption in your cash flow.

For example, a grant check that was due to come in today's mail is late. Normally this money comes in once a month, and has always been on time, yet, for whatever reason the check was mailed two days late. Unfortunately, your accounting department has already mailed a check to a vendor in anticipation of this deposit. Of course, there are other funds in the bank; yet, this money was allocated for a quarterly payroll tax payment that had to be in on time in order to avoid costly late penalties. If you have an overdraft account and the check comes in before the deposit does it will be paid. Your organization from time to time is going to need a safety net that comes in this form.

## Personal Nature

One of the most widely used sources of cash is the Family Loan. This intimate form of finance is generally low cost due to its personal nature, which can come from either your close friends or family. Of course, every aspect of the transaction must be handled in a professional manner using the same written provisions that are contained in a commercial loan. These types of loans generally are in the form of promissory notes. The repayment terms of these notes can be in any time interval that you deem necessary. The notes should follow *Generally Accepted Accounting Procedures* (GAAP). Once again, GAAP is discussed in the finance section. In general, any cash that comes into the organization should be clearly and unequivocally identifiable. Furthermore, all cash disbursements should always tie back to your general ledger. Once more, your bank and grantors will require that your finances be clean cut and easy to understand. Banks are very apprehensive of "spider web" accounting. The cash that flows in and out of the organization has to be accounted for in your annual independent financial audit.

# Chapter 10
# Finance and Accounting

The organization that you will create, or are presently running will be a direct reflection of how your finance and accounting functions are integrated throughout the company. For the most part, many businesses that have weak financial and accounting components simply do not survive, or experience problems with compliance and regulation. For that reason, your ability to develop and maintain a strong accounting department is crucial to your ability to run the organization profitably in the long term. In general, the financial processes that are employed within your company should correspond with *General Accepted Accounting Procedures* (GAAP). These accounting rules and regulations are designed to give outsiders, as well as, insiders a look into the financial health of your organization. CPA's, government accounting offices, Wall Street Firms, and most commercial banks use the procedures and rules that are employed by GAAP.

## Audited Financial Statement

All financial records that are kept should be maintained in a manner consistent with the principles that are outlined in these accounting rules. The majority of lenders and grant agencies are going to require that you submit a yearly audited financial statement. This audit will show the public where you received money and how you spent it during the last fiscal year.

## Dollars and Sense

The tool in which you will translate your goals and objectives to dollars and sense is the budget. This document is essentially a financial roadmap. Each budget usually contains all of the components that are necessary to run an organization for one year. The budget will contain fixed and variable costs that need to balance and tie out to your projected revenue. The basic premise behind budgeting is to always remain positively within the parameters set up on each general ledger (GL) line. Your budget should be realistic and manageable. And, by all means do not budget for services that you do not have the identifiable revenue in which to provide that service. The most fundamental rule of survival and growth is to control your costs. Quite simply, if you control your costs you will survive.

## Dollar for Dollar

The astute manager has to learn to gain the maximum return on each dollar that comes into the organization. Before any expenditure occurs, and even though you have budgeted for it, just ask yourself over and over again, do you really need to spend money right at this moment? Note that there are going to be times in which your expenses are going to exceed revenue and when that happens you must match or make a reallocation to each side of the balance sheet dollar for dollar. For example, the state has awarded you a grant for $600,000, which is $50,000 less than you requested, and there is not an identifiable way to replace that money—you must readjust your budget. Basically, you have to delay hiring that new counselor or purchasing that new ultrasound machine until you can identify some more cash. Figure 10-1 shows a budget that was not fully funded for one psychotherapist position.

## Future Health Organization, Inc.

## Revised Budget

## January 1, 2006 - December 31, 2006

|  |  | **CDBG** | **HHS** | **OTHER** | **TOTALS** |
|---|---|---|---|---|---|
| *Administration Salaries:* |  |  |  |  |  |
| Executive Director | 75,000 | 0 | 30,500 | 44,500 | 75,000 |
| Business Manager | 49,000 | 0 | 19,000 | 30,000 | 49,000 |
| Intake Supervisor | 25,000 | 0 | 10,500 | 14,500 | 25,000 |
| Physician | 46,020 | 11,450 | 11,450 | 23,120 | 46,020 |
| Nurse | 35,000 | 17,500 | 0 | 17,500 | 35,000 |
| Billing Clerk | 21,000 | 0 | 7,300 | 13,700 | 21,000 |
| Therapist (2)* | 100,000 | 0 | 0 | 50,000 | 50,000 |
| Admin. Asst. | 15,000 | 0 | 6,000 | 9,000 | 15,000 |
| Security PT | 7,500 | 500 | 3,700 | 3,300 | 7,500 |
| *Total Admin. Salaries:* | 373,520 | 29,450 | 88,450 | 205,620 | 323,520 |
| Fringe - 16% | 59,763 | 4,712 | 14,152 | 32,899 | 51,763 |
| **Total:** | **433,283** | **34,162** | **102,602** | **238,519** | **375,283** |
| *Consultants:* |  |  |  |  |  |
| Acct. Audit & Legal | 15,000 | 15,000 | 0 | 0 | 15,000 |
| **Total:** | **15,000** | **15,000** | **0** | **0** | **15,000** |
| *Space Cost:* |  |  |  |  |  |
| Facility Rentals | 12,000 | 0 | 6,000 | 6,000 | 12,000 |
| Utilities | 3,500 | 0 | 1,750 | 1,750 | 3,500 |
| Security System | 600 | 600 | 0 | 0 | 600 |
| Telephone | 7,000 | 2,500 | 4,500 | 0 | 7,000 |
| Insurance | 9,000 | 0 | 4,500 | 4,500 | 9,000 |
| Building Maint. | 1,000 | 0 | 500 | 500 | 1,000 |
| **Total:** | **33,100** | **3,100** | **17,250** | **12,750** | **33,100** |
| *Travel:* |  |  |  |  |  |
| Conference/Training | 250 | 125 | 0 | 125 | 250 |
| **Total:** | **250** | **125** | **0** | **125** | **250** |
| *Consumable Supplies:* |  |  |  |  |  |
| Office Supplies | 800 | 400 | 0 | 400 | 800 |
| Postage | 200 | 100 | 0 | 100 | 200 |
| **Total:** | **1,000** | **500** | **0** | **500** | **1,000** |
| *Equipment:* |  |  |  |  |  |
| Computers | 2,000 | 150 | 850 | 1,000 | 2,000 |
| Printers | 1,000 | 0 | 500 | 500 | 1,000 |
| **Total:** | **3,000** | **150** | **1,350** | **1,500** | **3,000** |

| Other Costs: | | | | | |
|---|---|---|---|---|---|
| Lab Services | 5,000 | 1,000 | 1,500 | 2,500 | 5,000 |
| Insurance - Other | 4,000 | 2,900 | 0 | 1,100 | 4,000 |
| Miscellaneous | 2,000 | 500 | 500 | 1,000 | 2,000 |
| Total Other: | 11,000 | 4,400 | 2,000 | 4,600 | 11,000 |
| | | | | | |
| TOTAL BUDGET: | **496,633** | **52,887** | **119,852** | **257,994** | **438,633** |

TOTAL ALL REVENUE: 438,633

*TOTAL (FAV/UNFAV)* (58,000)* Budget shortfall of $50,000 for (1) therapist plus fringes.

**FIGURE 10-1.** Predicted budget with funding shortfall.

In order to adjust the budget to meet the funding shortfall management is going to have to do either one or two things (1) scale back on the amount of predicted services, or (2) reallocate any funds that are unrestricted to the therapist line. Also, the amounts that are to be moved do not all have to come from the same line item. You may move a thousand here, and a thousand there, but, make sure that your accounting is clean. It should always be easy to explain specific changes to your budget. Remember no spider web accounting.

# Financial Integrity

The general accounting manual that follows is designed to immediately put into place internal controls, that if followed will maintain the financial integrity of your books. The organization's financial accounting structure must conform to GAAP at all times. In fact, your outside auditor is going to want to take a look at these procedures and where applicable, conduct random tests of these controls. Upon completion of a thorough audit, the outside accountants are going to present to management a list of findings. These findings can be good or bad depending on what the auditors uncover in their examination of your financial records. As a matter of good practice your records should be keep in a safe and secure place accessible only to those authorized personnel. The records that you maintain such as billing, accounts payable and receivable should be stored according to the policy of the governing source. For instance, Medicare billing records must be maintained for a certain number of years before they can be destroyed. The record retention time limits for third party payers will be conveyed to you during the initial contracting phase. In addition, your local, state and Federal Departments of Health will also have a retention policy applicable for your facility. Again, as the director of the organization you are solely responsible for compliance and thus should familiarize yourself with these guidelines.

## Financial Health

After senior management has had an opportunity to address the findings in the audit, your Board of Directors must also be made aware of any material findings, and must subsequently approve management's corrective action in regards to the findings. Your goal is to ensure that this document accurately states the organizations' financial health during a specific period of time, which is usually one year. This audit will be used by your bank and is normally requested as a part of any grant application. In fact, in the audit you have to list all grants that have been received within that period. This documentation is usually necessary for a funding source to: (a) establish a grant history, and (b) have certified proof that you have spent your funding in an acceptable manner. The sample finance manual that follows is a good start to your overall collection of policies and procedures. However, you will probably need to make adjustments to certain sections depending on your type of operation and licensing stipulations.

## Hamilton Health Care, Inc.
General Accounting Manual

### Accounting Department
SUBJECT:    Chart of Accounts

Background

Hamilton Health Care, Inc., (HH) will maintain a chart of accounts that identifies sources of revenue and expense accounts. All grants will be clearly identified and any expenditures will be clearly discernible by using grant codes. All revenue will be identified as being restricted or unrestricted. At no time shall any of those funds be commingled in one common fund.

### Purchase Order System
SUBJECT:    Purchase Orders

Background

Purchase orders (PO) must be approved by the FINANCE MANAGER or his/her designate prior to making an order. All non-contract materials must be ordered via purchase orders.

Procedure

1. HH purchase orders must be filled out by the individual requesting same.
2. Purchase orders must be approved and signed by the FINANCE MANAGER or his/her designate.
3. Upon arrival the order must be compared to the original PO. Any discrepancies must be immediately noted.
4. The purchase order and the packing slip will be compared by the FINANCE MANAGER for submittal to accounting for payment.

Purchasing Equipment and Supplies

Prior to purchasing any equipment or supplies, you must review the appropriate program budget to verify that the item and/or sufficient funds are included in the budget. If you are not sure, please contact your program assistant or staff accounting. Also, you should be aware of purchasing restrictions dictated by certain funding sources, and remember that no purchases are to take place without permission from the FINANCE MANAGER or his/her designate.

*Remember*: HH does not pay sales tax. Be sure to take a tax-exempt form to give to all vendors whenever making a purchase. Also, please note that we must have written bids on the vendor's letterhead for services and goods with a value of $1000 or more.

*Special Note*: It must be stressed that whether, or not, you order an item through your office or through the central office; a packing slip is required to pay invoices. Invoices cannot be paid without proof of delivery. <u>PLEASE BE AWARE THAT YOU MUST RECEIVE A PACKING SLIP WITH ALL DELIVERIES.</u> If you misplace a packing slip, you must attach a note indicating that a packing slip is not available, noting the list of items received and immediately forward it to the appropriate person upon delivery.

## INVENTORY CONTROL

The administrative office will maintain a list of all corporate equipment. The following information will be kept on file:

- ✓ Item
- ✓ Description
- ✓ Model number
- ✓ Serial number
- ✓ Location

## PRINTING REQUEST

When ordering stationary, envelopes or any printed matter, you must complete a purchase order, and forward it to the Administration Office. Please attach a clean sample of what you need.

Administrative

Policy/Procedures Statement

Release of Information

SUBJECT:     Release of financial or statistical information

Background

To control the release of financial or statistical information to banks, outside agencies, or to authorized individuals. Some requests require completion of a form with specific information about Hamilton Health Care, Inc.

Written Requests

If the request is by letter or requires the completion of a form or other document, the material is to be forwarded to either the Finance Manager, Corporate Treasurer or Board Secretary who will then decide what information may be released and who will be authorized to reply.

Verbal Requests

If the request is made by a personal visit to our office, the requester will be referred directly to the Finance Manager. If by telephone, the call should be transferred to the Finance Manager. If the call cannot be transferred, the person receiving the call should obtain the caller's name, company, telephone number and address if possible. In addition, obtain the reason for the request, a brief description of the information asked for, and the name of the person taking the call. The information obtained is to be forwarded to the Finance Manager immediately for follow-up and reply.

Administrative

Policy / Procedure Statement

Furniture and Equipment

SUBJECT:   Furniture and Equipment Control Procedures

Background

The purpose of maintaining the furniture and equipment inventory is to comply with general accepted accounting principles.

Responsibility

Department heads are responsible and accountable for all furniture and equipment in their department and they are to maintain some type of control over furniture and equipment. Property accounting will assist in and evaluate any department's furniture and equipment inventory control procedures.

Purchase of Furniture and Equipment

Furniture and equipment purchased will be recorded and kept on file.

Stolen Property

Furniture and equipment that is missing or has been stolen will be reported in writing to the security department as soon as possible. The description, serial number, inventory number, and other information about the lost item should be included in the report.

## Temporary Transfer of Property

The loan or transfer of furniture and equipment between departments for short periods need not be reported to administration. However, the department head to which the property is assigned will be held accountable for the loaned item and should, for protection, require a memorandum receipt for furniture or equipment loaned to another department. This receipt should be available for presentation when requested.

## Permanent Interdepartmental Transfers

Interdepartmental transfers will be reported to administration in writing including the description, serial number, inventory number of the property being transferred, the name of the department to receive the property and proof that the department has received the property. Administration will assist in transferring furniture or equipment from one department to another. The department head to whom it was assigned to originally will be held accountable until property accounting is notified of the transfer. After being notified, the department head acquiring the property assumes accountability.

## Audit of Department's Inventory

Each department's inventory will be audited periodically by property accounting. A report of this audit will be sent to the Finance Manager or his/her designate.

Administrative

Policy / Procedure Statement

Cash Receipts Procedures

SUBJECT:   Banking Policy

Background

Management shall ensure that all cash receipts shall be safeguarded and accounted for in a manner consistent with Generally Accepted Accounting Principles (GAAP). All finance employees will follow the appropriate procedures for processing cash receipt transactions. Hamilton maintains accounts at Any National Bank. Any National Bank maintains the following accounts:

1. Operating Account - All accounts payable vouchers are paid from this account.
2. Imprest Account - Petty Cash account.
3. Payroll Account - The payroll account is maintained on an imprest basis.

   A. *Establishing Bank Accounts* – All bank accounts that are opened must be approved by the Corporate Treasurer. Each bank account must contain the corporate name, tax identification number and must appear on the organization general ledger.

   B. *Deposits to Bank Account* – All cash receipts are to be deposited into this account. Including patient payments, insurance company checks and refunds. A deposit slip must be completed and filled out by someone other than the person who opens the mail.

C. *Mail Receipts Reconciliation and Posting* – The mail opener receives the business office mail and opens those letters that appear to be checks. The checks are then immediately endorsed and copied. The check information is immediately added to the daily cash receipts report. All checks along with an adding machine tape of all receipts are forwarded to the business office manager for deposit slip preparation. Once the bank has validated the deposit, it should then be returned to the original letter opener. At that point the letter opener should initial the cash receipts report. The business office manager shall be notified at once if there are any discrepancies.

Administrative

Policy / Procedure Statement

Employee's Time Records

SUBJECT:   Payroll

Background

All employees shall maintain either time sheets or time cards. No exceptions. All interns required by their institutions shall also maintain time records. All employee time records will identify the source of revenue from which they are to be paid from.

Procedures

Employees will either punch in and out or sign in and out on a daily basis. Supervisors will check this and sign completed time sheets on a weekly basis.

Administrative

Policy / Procedure Statement

Bi-Weekly Payroll Reports

SUBJECT:     Payroll

Background

HH will maintain a record of all personnel payments for a period not to exceed five (5) years or the minimum allowed by the state division of labor and employment.

Procedures

Payroll reports will be forwarded to the accounting office for approval and subsequently filed in a binder for future use.

Administrative

Policy / Procedure Statement

Employee Expenses

SUBJECT:     Travel Procedures

Background

Employees of Hamilton Health Care, Inc., are reimbursed for reasonable and necessary expenses incurred while in the performance of approved travel.

AUTHORIZATION FOR OFFICIAL TRAVEL

Each employee required to travel in performance of official duties and entitled to reimbursement for expenses incurred shall have prior authorization from the executive director.

Required Approval

The approval requirements of travel are as follows:

A. In-State and Out-of-State Business trips require approval of immediate supervisor.
B. In-State and Out-of-State trips for conferences, conventions, associations and meetings require approval of the Finance Manager.

Advance Payment - Conference Registration Fees

In order, to pay registration fees in advance of any conference, these procedures must be followed:

The request should be made at least 20 days in advance of the start of the conference.

The request should be made on a remittance voucher form with both the literature concerning the conference and required approval signature.

## Advance Payment - Airline Travel

To pay airline travel in advance of the conference, these procedures must be followed:

Travel times and destinations must be submitted by the employee at least 20 days in advance of the start of conference. Travel arrangements and airline reservations will be made by the employee at the lowest cost the health center.

## Reimbursement of Travel Expense

### General

Travel Vouchers received by administration will be processed as soon as possible provided there are no problems with the voucher.

### Expense Reimbursement

Immediately upon returning from a trip, the traveler should submit a voucher for reimbursement of travel expenses. If not, within 30 days of the return, any advance received will be deducted from the traveler's paycheck the next pay period. The first two copies of the travel voucher, with required receipts attached, should be completed as outlined in the attachment hereto and submitted to administration. Vouchers submitted with error other than mathematical errors will be returned. Travel expenses will be reimbursed only for the employee's own expense. One employee cannot submit expenses for reimbursement on the same voucher with another person.

## Reimbursement for Meals

Reimbursements for meals will be for actual expenditure (plus tips) at a reasonable amount with receipts attached.

## Day Trips

No reimbursement is authorized for meals when travel in confined to the vicinity of your home. For other travel, reimbursement for meals shall be:

> *Breakfast* - when travel begins before 6:00 AM and extends beyond 8:00 AM.
>
> *Lunch* - when travel begins before 12:00 PM and extends beyond 2:00 PM.
>
> *Dinner* - when travel extends beyond 8:00 PM.

No reimbursement is authorized for a dinner meal when the meeting is completed in sufficient time for travel to return by 6:00 PM.

## Lodging Expenses

Reimbursement will be made for lodging expense incurred in a hotel or motel upon the presentation of a paid original bill. When a room is shared with other employees on travel status, reimbursement will be calculated on a prorated share of the total cost. The other traveler must submit a copy of the lodging receipt indicating that the room was shared. An employee on travel status, if accompanied by a spouse that is not an employee on travel status, is entitled to reimbursement at the single room rate. Request that the hotel clerk note the single room rate of the bill.

Normally, if the first order of business for which the travel was authorized begins after 3PM, reimbursement will not be made for lodging prior to the first day of business. However, an exception will be made should the order of business begin prior to 3PM and lodging is necessary for the traveler to be present for the first order of business. Reimbursement is made for lodging the final evening of the trip if the traveler is not able to return home by 9PM.

Modes of Transportation

Transportation authorized for official travel includes health care vehicles, private vehicles, common carriers, and rental cars.

If travel is by other than the most direct route between points where official health care business is conducted, the additional cost must be borne by the traveler. No traveler can claim transportation expenses where another person gratuitously transports him, or when he is transported by another traveler who is entitled to reimbursement for transportation expense. Private vehicle mileage reimbursement cannot exceed cost of round trip air coach fare.

Private vehicle

The Employee shall receive the legal rate established by the Internal Revenue Service for each mile actually and necessarily traveled in the performance of official duties.

*The following situations justify the use of private vehicle for travel*:

1. When travel is required at such time or to such places that common carrier transportation may not be reasonably available.

2. When one or more persons travel to the same destination in the same car and total mileage claimed does not exceed the total airline coach fares for transporting the same number of people.

# Chapter 11
# Marketing

The identity of your organization is perhaps it's most valuable component. And always remember that the most important asset you will possess is your good name. Furthermore, it must be protected and cultivated, each and every day that you operate. This is true for several reasons. First and foremost, a donor is extremely unlikely to give money to an organization that is mired in scandal, or plagued with negative headlines in the local newspaper. As outlined in the business plan there is going to have be a constant effort on your part to ensure that the community is well aware of the good things that are going on in your agency in a consistent manner. The significance of this effort is to make sure that donors are constantly reminded that you are providing services that are visible and necessary to a chosen population. Your intention is to compel those individuals and companies who would like to give a donation a persuasive reason to give to your organization.

## Right Of Entry

Indeed, those organizations that consistently market themselves to the community in a positive manner experience very little resistance when it comes to soliciting donations. Marketing your agency can be done in several ways. And, as a non-profit you have a right of entry to resources that for-profits cannot access. For instance, some of the largest advertising companies in America have programs developed just to assist organizations in the community who are non-profit. Were you aware that the outdoor advertisement industry is able to furnish a full sized billboard for little or no cost? In fact, in some cases they'll help you to develop the content to feature in the outdoor ad.

Just imagine the impact that your agency will have on the community when it sees your name on top of a large building with letters that are 5-10 feet tall. The cable industry also has many cooperative programs that will allow you to run 20-30 second advertisements during certain non-peak segments. You can expedite this process by going to your local trade school that teaches students the art of film and television production. Many of these professors and students are always looking for creative projects. After contacting the administrators of the school and letting them know that you want to make a short public service announcement, more than likely they will approve the project without cost to your organization. This partnership benefits both the school and the community and the students will have a great time.

## Airspace

The next marketing venue to consider would be the airways. Radio stations are normally very receptive to community segments. In reality, many stations have staff members assigned to assist non-profits in their efforts to get their perspective messages out to the community. However, given the fact that airspace is very expensive as are the operational aspects of most stations, you can improve your success of getting on the air if you have a media firm put together a completed "spot" for you in the customary format ready for delivery to the station. What's more, there are ready, willing and able public relations firm that may do the media work pro bono.

## In-house Marketing

The most successful tried and true form of advertising has always been by "word of mouth." This method of communication is quite effective and should be the primary technique that your organization employs to build up and maintain your volume. It is a fact that many clients and patients make a great number of referrals to their service providers. These personal attestations are both priceless and very effective. Therefore, each client must be seen as a potential reference source. Each staff member in your office must be trained to deliver the highest possible level of service. This above and beyond effort will inevitably lead to increased patient satisfaction. Once your patient satisfaction level goes up your referrals will follow along the scale. If truth were told, it is a superb idea to make sure that you are always asking your clients for referrals. You'll be surprised that many of them will be glad to help you in your efforts to grow. In some instances there will be a few people that will feel a sense of satisfaction in the thought that they contributed to your success.

## Pick Up The Phone

The person responsible for new admissions should develop a phone schedule that will be used to call patients that are new and those that have come in once or twice and have not returned. This is a quick source of potential patient revenue without spending any up front money. A sample telephone script can be used similar to the one seen here in figure 11-1.

## In-House Telemarketing Script

Hello, (patient's or client's name), my name is (caller), and I'm calling from Global Health Care. The (doctor/therapist) asked me to call you because you haven't been in for your regular appointment.

He/she is concerned because you may not have had any medical/counseling treatment since you completed your examination here at the center. And, that you may be having some problems associated, and related to your initial examination here at our office.

Our doctor/therapist wants to make sure that if you're having a problem, we can help you in the early stages, before any irreversible damage can occur. And, you will be glad to know that he feels so strongly about it that he's authorized me to set aside a free gift for you. Just remember to mention, when you come in, that (caller) told you that a gift has been set aside to thank you for coming in. How about (day, date & time)? Or (day, date & time)?

**How to over come common objections**

1. "No, that's not a good time for me..."
REPLY: I can make you an appointment for (day, date & time)...

2. "It's inconvenient to make the trip to your office..."
REPLY: We are conveniently located on Gooden Street between Easy Does It and Wellborn Way. The buses that come by here are the Local Newport, Local Exchange Place, #28, Mystical Park, and

NICE Science Center. I can make you an appointment for (day, date & time)...

3. "I'll think about it and let you know..."
REPLY: We are very concerned about you because you have been out of treatment already for so long. It is very important for your health, and well being to begin treatment immediately. I can make you an appointment for (day, date & time)...

4. "Your office staff is very uncooperative..."
REPLY: You'll be glad to know that we have implemented mandatory education and training requirements for our staff. They have also been trained to be courteous and sensitive to the needs of our clients. I can make you an appointment for (day, date & time)...

5. "I'm presently going to another center for treatment..."
REPLY: We are happy that you are receiving treatment. May I ask why you stopped coming to our center?"
NOTE: ALWAYS BE COURTEOUS AND PROFESSIONAL

**FIGURE 11-1**. Telephone Script.

# Fee for Service

The next task in your marketing strategy should be for the organization to identify all services that can be marketed to outside companies and government agencies. This strategy provides for an excellent source of steady income that is not dependent on internal patient flow or volume. There are several key human resource functions that many companies outsource to sub-contractors. Some of the tasks that can be done by your organization can include physical examinations, drug testing and employee assistance program (EAP) services.

## Employee Assistance Services

Companies that outsource these services are school bus companies, local social security offices, Federal immigration offices, local school boards, and trucking companies just to name a few. For instance, your local social security office is responsible for evaluating hundreds of people each year to determine eligibility to receive disability benefits. This office generally will need to contract with a local provider that can perform any number of services. These services include psychiatric screening, which must be performed by a licensed psychiatrist, pediatric examinations, performed by a licensed pediatrician, pulmonary testing, and full internal medicine examinations, again performed by a licensed physician. These services are extremely profitable and the payment time is very fast. Once the examining physician does the dictation a check is automatically generated by the computer system. Depending on the service provided such as a full psychiatric examination the remittance can range anywhere from $75-$90. So, if there are 20 examinations performed on a given week, it would not be surprising to find 20 checks in the mail the very next week. However, keep in mind that the services that are performed at your organization must be of the highest quality. The individuals that come into your office for an examination should be treated with the utmost courtesy. It is not the responsibility of your office staff to determine whether or not this person will receive benefits, your organization is just performing an independent service. Thus, the client should be treated in the same manner as the rest of the folks sitting in the waiting room waiting to be seen for their prospective appointment.

The board of education in many towns and municipalities are accountable for the transportation of a certain number of school children throughout the year. Many of these boards have drivers that are required to submit to physical examinations that include drug testing. In fact, the Omnibus Transportation Employee Testing Act of 1991 necessitates drug and alcohol testing of safety-sensitive transportation employees working in trucking, mass transit, aviation, pipelines, railroads, and other transportation industries.

## Drug and Alcohol Testing Services

The Federal Department of Transportation (DOT) publishes rules on who must conduct drug and alcohol tests and what procedures to use when administering these tests. Specifically, regulations 49 CFR, PART 40 and PART 382 state in part that employers must provide certified proof of compliance upon inspection of their employee records that the company has in fact randomly tested a certain percentage of eligible employees for substance abuse and for alcohol use. The percentage of employees tested for drugs can range from 50% to 25%. And, those employees tested for alcohol will be 10%. The employer must also have a program in place to test new hires and provisions in place to test an employee after an accident has occurred. In effect, in order for a company to prove that it is in compliance with these transportation rules they will require you to provide an attestation such as the one in figure 11-2.

*Matt Hamilton, MBA, Ph.D.*

## **DOT Attestation Letter**

October 18, 2004

Danielle Winchester, Manager
Top School Bus Company, Inc.
456 Federal Avenue
Chicago, IL 60619

Dear Ms. Winchester:

This letter is an attestation certifying that your company has an active contract with Hamilton Health Care Company, a Connecticut Counseling Facility licensed to provide Primary Care and Drug Abuse Treatment Services. This contract covers your employees for drug and alcohol testing as well as EAP services.

The testing that is performed complies fully with United States Department of Transportation Regulations 49 CFR, PART 40 and PART 382. The test used is a five (5) panel DOT Drug Screen.

In addition, your company is also in compliance with the Omnibus Transportation Employee Testing Act of 1991. This act requires alcohol testing of safety-sensitive employees in the aviation, motor carrier, mass transit and railroad industries.

_____                                        _____
Danielle Winchester                                                                                         Date
Manager

State of Connecticut         )
                                          )      ss:
County of Eastern             )

On this 18th day of October, 2004, Before me personally came and appeared Danielle Winchester, known, and known to me, to be the individual described in and who executed the foregoing instrument, and who duly acknowledged to me the he executed same for the purpose therein contained.

In witness whereof, I hereunto set my hand and official seal.

_____

Notary Public

My commission expires:_____

**FIGURE 11-2**. DOT Testing Compliance Letter.

As you can see there is a significant amount of testing to be done on a yearly basis that can increase your cash flow in lieu of grants. However, you must be prepared to contact these businesses on a consistent basis. For the most part, the local phone book will contain a directory of transportation companies that you can start with right away. A good sales letter (figure 11-3) stating your intentions should be sent to these companies and followed up with a phone call to management. Conversely, many of these companies are aware of the transportation rules, but many are out of compliance. The problem is that many companies take a wait and see attitude on the matter. In other words, some take a chance that they will not be inspected, and will not take a proactive step unless they are compelled to do so. Also, there are those companies that do have a degree of trouble interpreting the rules. This provides you with an excellent opportunity to sell a complete testing and compliance program.

*Matt Hamilton, MBA, Ph.D.*

## Sample Sales Letter
## Employee Assistance Program & Drug Testing Services

October 15, 2004

VIA FAX (123 456-7890) AND US MAIL

Big Top, Office Manager

Union Contractors and Coalition of Trade Workers

255 Anywhere Street

Anyplace, USA 12345

Dear Ms. Top:

Thank you in advance for the opportunity to assist your company in achieving your goal of a Drug Free Work Place. We have an intensive and thorough random drug testing system that will enable your company to hire and maintain substance free employees. Specifically, the idea is to protect your company's officers and assets from theft, accidents and non-compliance on Federal, New England State and local contracts, as it relates to mandatory substance abuse testing for employees in a safety sensitive position. And, as I mentioned in our conversation, test results can be obtained within 24 hours.

We are a fully licensed organization located right in your neighborhood. We have the facilities, and medical staff to handle all of your substance abuse testing to include DOT transportation requirements including physicals for Commercial Drivers License (CDL).

As I stated in our conversation, we will assist you in putting together a written policy for testing your employees. This will ensure that your company is protected. In addition, we will provide the following services:

1. Conduct random urine, and alcohol screens for all CDL and <u>safety sensitive employees</u> of the above mentioned company in accordance with Department of Transportation (DOT) regulations, 49 CFR, PART 40 and PART 382, whereas employers must provide certified proof of compliance upon inspection and;

2. Provide all supplies and supervise specimen collections at our new location 587 Anywhere Avenue, New Town, MA and;

3. Negative test results will be available 24 hours after collection. Positive results will be re-tested and results made available within 48 hours and;

4. Should an employee test result come back positive for an illegal substance, HAMILTON will accept that employee into the EAP for treatment provided that the employer agrees to do so, the decision to retain the employee is the sole responsibility of the employer and;

5. Urine testing will be 5 Panel Drug Screens for <u>$40.00</u> per test and;

6. Provide employment physicals for a flat rate of <u>$50.00</u> which includes (1) examination, (2) TB test and (3) specific gravity urinalysis and;

7. Provide a combination of the Drug Screen and Physical Examination for a flat price of <u>$70.00</u> and;

8. HAMILTON will provide test results to management with the understanding that HAMILTON is not responsible for any disciplinary ac-

tions that may or may not result from a positive or negative test result and;

9. Employer will pay for all fees in advance until a credit account has been established and;

10. Furthermore, do to the sensitive nature of drug testing the employer must identify those individuals within the organization who will be privy to test results and other sensitive information regarding employees.

The primary point to remember is that HAMILTON has strict policies regarding security and confidentiality. HAMILTON will only report drug-testing information to specific personnel designated by your company. Access to this confidential information is limited both internally and externally. We look forward to assisting you in ensuring that you obtain and maintain a drug-free work environment. However, should an emergency come up, and you need any of our services, I have made our staff aware of our impending association. Should you have any further questions, please do not hesitate to call me at (123) 456-7890.

With warm regards,

Your Name,
Office Manager

**FIGURE 11-3**. Sales (DOT) Letter.

Now, once you do win a contract you can follow the example in figure 11-4 to send over an agreement to your new customer.

## **EMPLOYEE ASSISTANCE PLAN AGREEMENT**

The parties of this agreement are <u>Big School Incorporated</u>, located at 654 Good News Avenue, Freehold, NY referred to as the employer, and Hamilton Health Care Corporation, located at 213 West Easy Street, Long Island, NY referred to as (HAMILTON). This agreement will be for one year beginning October 20, 2004 and ending October 20, 2005.

Hamilton Health Care, Inc., will perform the following services:

1. Conduct random urine, and alcohol screens for all CDL and safety sensitive workers of the above mentioned company in accordance with Department of Transportation (DOT) regulations, 49 CFR, PART 40 and PART 382 effective January 1, 1996, whereas employers must provide certified proof of compliance upon inspection and;

2. As per DOT regulations randomly test fifty (50) percent of eligible employees for substance abuse, and twenty five (25) percent for alcohol abuse and;

3. Provide all supplies and supervise specimen collections at our clinic located at 213 West Easy Street, Long Island, NY and;

4. Negative test results will be available 24 hours after collection. Positive results will be retested and results made available within 48 hours and;

5. Should an employee test result come back positive for an illegal substance, HAMILTON will accept that employee into the EAP for treat-

ment provided that the employer agrees to do so, the decision to retain the employee is the sole responsibility of the employer and;

6. Urine testing will be 5 Panel DOT Drug Screens for $25.00 per test and;

7. Provide alcohol breath testing for $25.00 per test and;

8. Provide Pre-employment physicals for a flat rate of $50.00 which includes (1) examination, (2) TB test and (3) specific gravity urinalysis and;

9. HAMILTON will provide test results to management with the understanding that is not responsible for any disciplinary actions that may or may not result from a positive or negative test result and;

10. HAMILTON will charge the employer a flat rate per test. HAMILTON will invoice the employer on a monthly basis and;

11. HAMILTON will provide a random list of employees who are to be tested and when they should be tested to the employer at least 24 hours before hand. Furthermore, do to the sensitive nature of drug testing the employer must identify those individuals within the organization who will be privy to test results and other sensitive information regarding employees.

12. In addition, should HAMILTON for any reason fail to perform any of the agreed upon tasks, the employer, upon notice to HAMILTON and opportunity to correct can void the agreement with 30 days notice.

SIGNATURE                                                              DATE

_____                          _____

BIG SCHOOL, INC.

Authorized Representative


_____                          _____

HAMILTON HEALTH CARE

Authorized Representative

**FIGURE 11-4.** DOT Testing Agreement.

# Chapter 12
# Staffing

## Paid Employees

The staffing requirements in a non-profit are not much different than those in a for-profit business. The distinction between the two entities is found in the mission and the philosophy of each entity. An employee that is hired to work at a for-profit company is often driven by organizational goals that focus primarily on investor returns in the form of quarterly profits and guided financial ratios. Conversely, the employee that will be attracted to your business will be motivated by the idea of helping others. This employee is motivated by their desire to serve other people. Money is not their primary driver. Yet, of course, they do also expect fair and timely compensation for their hard work. Whereas, the employee that works in a for-profit company may move from job to job, in a conscious effort to reach a higher pay scale. Hence, altruism is secondary. As outlined and discussed in the communications chapter it is management's responsibility to ensure that this good will employee is recognized for their unselfish and humane work.

This is especially vital in that many employees that work for non-profits are not paid as much as their peers that work in for-profit enterprises. As a consequence, it is imperative that these employees are compensated in other ways such as pleasant working environments, and where possible, flexible working hours and plenty of healthy recognition.

## Counseling And Psychotherapy

The organization whose areas of focus are counseling and psychotherapy will want to hire an extensive variety of healthcare providers. The range of experience will vary from the mom who is starting a new career and has absolutely no clue about counseling whatsoever, to former and present police officers. Now, at the other end of the spectrum you should have access to a licensed psychiatrist, a licensed psychologist at both the Masters and Doctoral levels, licensed nurses, licensed professional counselors, social workers, substance abuse counselors, both certified and uncertified such as college interns. As a matter of fact, you can staff the front office with volunteers. There is a substantial pool of students and retired persons who would be more than willing to answer phones, and to make up charts for your professional staff.

## Volunteers

Additionally, you may want to apply to become a sponsor for AmeriCorps Volunteers In Service To America (VISTA). VISTA Volunteers can serve at least one year of full-time service with local, state, and federal agencies, public, private, and faith-based nonprofit organizations. The purpose is to address the needs of low-income American communities. The range of projects can be from building permanent infrastructure in nonprofit organizations to doing healthcare outreach in communities suffering from poverty. AmeriCorps is a wonderful program and can be very beneficial to your organization both in terms of bringing community people on board who are interested in making your organization work in a heartfelt manner; and, the fact that the members are paid a stipend by VISTA for the one-year that they remain at your site. The obligation that the organization has comes in the form of supervision, space, phone, equipment, and service-related travel. In other words, you have to invest your time to manage and train these eager volunteers. In an effort to assist you in managing these volunteers there is a section in the personnel policy manual regarding supervision of these unpaid helpers. And, keep in mind that the more success that your organization has with these initial volunteers, VISTA will provide more resources to help your organization participate successfully in the Faith-Based and Community Initiative (FBCI). This is not a distinct program and the entry points are through three main government entities namely Senior Corps, AmeriCorps, and Learn and Serve America. These agencies have numerous grants available for a wide range of community issues. For example, Substance Abuse and Mental Health Services Administration (SAMHSA) will administer over $100 million dollars for one year of grant funding for an assortment of programs throughout the United States.

# Physician Recruiting – *Making the case for a Visa in a Health Profession Shortage Area*

One of the most difficult staffing positions to fill in any non-profit is that of the primary care physician. An Internal Medicine physician salary for a community organization can reach as high as $150,000 on average. One of the best avenues available to the non-profit is the International Medical School Graduate. These physicians are in the United States attending medical school and must leave the country upon completion of their residencies. However, many of these doctors are interested in practicing medicine in America. And, they have good reasons for wanting to do so. The opportunities for employment and the use of new technology in this country are obviously greater here than in their countries of origin for many of these bright graduates. However, the Immigration and Naturalization Service (INS) has very strict rules regarding holders of temporary visas. The medical student generally attends school on a limited F-1 student visa. Further, the student that has relatives such as a spouse can subsequently be issued a lower derivative of that particular visa such as F-2, J-2 or H-4.

## H-1B1

The medical student that wishes to stay in the country must be sponsored and apply for a different visa status such as the H-1B1. Yet, currently the United States will only issue a maximum of 65,000 of these "specialty occupation" visas. This visa is issued for a period of three years, but may be extended. In addition, the visa holder can also apply for a green card if the organization wants to sponsor the application. The 65,000 visas are allocated among various specialties that include accounting, architects, computer analysts, computer programmers, database administrators, web designers, engineers, financial analysts, doctors, nurses, scientists, and lawyers. Therefore, the petition that is submitted on behalf of this immigrant by the employer is subject to numerical limitations. Each occupation is assigned a specific number of visas based upon detailed needs of the United States economy. And, once that numerical milestone has been reached there will not be any new visas issued until the next year.

What is the alternative for the physician if all of the slots are allocated? The rules of immigration state that in some instances should the individual leave the country he or she may not return to the US for a specified period of time. And, in some instances for up to 10 years, depending on their specific country. The alternative for the doctor is to apply early in their training to a specific internship in a hospital so that he can specialize in perhaps neurological medicine. This internship may last for another 4 years or more. But, if there are no internships available the doctor must prepare to leave the country according to immigration law.

# Health Profession Shortage Area

There is another option available in the form of community service in a Health Profession Shortage Area. Nonetheless, even after the organization and the physician successfully maneuver through the tumultuous process of applying for this waiver, there are no guarantees that the INS will allow the physician to remain in the country. In spite of that, most applicants that are processed all the way through the system usually are granted the waiver. The process of applying for the waiver is twofold. The organization has its piece, and the physician will have his part. And, each partner will have expenses that come in the form of fees and paperwork. In the end, both sides of the partnership must complete all tasks and meet all applicable requirements. Many physicians and non-profit administrators are not aware of the steps necessary to successfully apply for a job in a health profession shortage area. Thus, this section of the book contains most of the information that is necessary to fill out applications at the Federal and state levels. Also, in this section, you will find that certain data is going to have to be compiled and submitted to various entities including the physician's immigration lawyer.

In general, after the graduate has been offered employment a written "Employment Offer" is signed by both parties as seen in figure 12-1.

## Sample Employment Offer Letter

May 1, 2004

John Doe, MD
Good Life Road
Pleasant, AZ 85001

Dear Dr. Doe:

This letter will confirm the offer of employment made to you by our company. We are pleased to offer you the position of Physician (Internal Medicine). Your compensation will be $105,000 paid bi-weekly and we have included additional incentives in your employment contract. The enclosed contract is for a period of three (3) years.

This offer is conditional upon approval by INS of your H-1B1 VISA waiver application.

We understand that you will advise us on whether you will accept this position by May 5, 2004 and that, if you do accept will start work by July 1, 2004.

We look forward to you joining our organization and are confident that we shall have a long mutually rewarding relationship.

Very truly,

Executive Director

**FIGURE 12-1.** Offer of Employment.

## Labor Attestation

In addition, to the letter of employment you must also prepare a binding contract like the one shown in figure 12-2. These documents are going to be used when you file a *Labor Attestation* as the employer of an H-1B1 professional. Also, the agreement must spell out specifically the qualifications and duties of staff membership as indicated in appendix A & B. Lastly, an agreement must be signed by the physician to allow your organization to submit requests for payment on behalf of the physician for services rendered at your facility (Appendix C).

# EMPLOYMENT AGREEMENT

THIS EMPLOYMENT AGREEMENT, made this <u>3rd</u> day of <u>May 2004</u> by and between <u>John Doe, MD</u> (hereinafter referred to as "Physician"); and Jordan Health Care, Inc., Pleasant, AZ 85001, (hereinafter referred to as JORDAN);

WHEREAS, <u>John Doe, MD</u> is fully licensed and qualified to practice <u>Internal Medicine</u> in the State of Arizona and has met the qualifications and duties as defined in (APPENDIX A); and,

WHEREAS, JORDAN is in the business of offering healthcare services to patients and seeks to engage Physician to serve as a (n) <u>Family Practioner</u> at JORDAN's Ambulatory Facility.

WHEREAS, Physician desires to be employed by JORDAN in said capacity upon the terms and conditions hereinafter set forth;

NOW, THEREFORE, in consideration for the mutual covenants and conditions set forth within this Contract, it is agreed by and between the parties hereto as follows:

1. AUTHORITY:

1.1 In accordance with JORDAN corporate objectives, procedures and Mission Statement, the Physician will conduct those activities necessary to fulfill the requirements as specified in the job description.

2. TERM:

2.1 This Employment Agreement shall commence on the date and year first above noted and shall continue in full force and effect for a term of 3 years to end on May 31, 2007 subject, however, to prior termination as hereinafter provided.

3. RENEWAL:

3.1 The term of this Agreement shall automatically renew for successive periods of one (1) year unless either party shall have delivered written notice to the other party at least thirty (30) days prior to the expiration of the initial term or any renewal term, that such party does not intend to renew this Agreement.

4. SCOPE AND DEFINITION OF DUTIES:

4.1 Physician agrees to provide professional services to JORDAN as described in (APPENDIX B) entitled Duties of Physician, which is attached hereto and made a part of hereof. Said services shall be provided in accordance with the high professional standards of JORDAN as set forth in the Personnel and Operating Manual.

(a) Physician shall be responsible to work three (3) clinical sessions per week. One clinical session is defined as uninterrupted 12 hours of clinical duties. Assignment of clinical sessions shall be the responsibility of the Clinic Director and shall be in the best interests of patient care.

5. COMPENSATION:

5.1     Salary: During the first year of this Agreement, JORDAN shall pay the Physician the annual sum of $105,000.00 for the period of the contract, to be paid in bi-weekly installments which shall be in consideration of Physician's services which shall be equal to 1,872 hours per year.

5.2     Benefits: Physician shall receive as compensation from JORDAN benefits according to the following schedule:

Vacation:       30
Sick Days:      5
CME Conferences: 7
Insurance:      Major Medical and Dental Coverage and Malpractice.

5.3     Physician shall comply with all JORDAN Human Resources policies and procedures, rules and regulations.

5.4     All billings for the professional services of the Physician will be assigned to and be the responsibility of JORDAN (Appendix C). Physician shall promptly deliver all claims for professional services to JORDAN and JORDAN shall have rights to all fees for all professional services rendered by Physician pursuant to the terms of this Agreement.

6.      DISCRETION IN FIXING SALARIES AND INCREASES IN SALARIES:

6.1     JORDAN anticipates maintaining the salary structure as outlined in the foregoing section. After the first year of service, actual increases in salary shall be based upon the quality of work and performance.

7. HONORARIUMS AND ROYALTIES:

7.1 Monies and other things of value received by Physician by way of honorariums and royalties shall be considered personal income of Physician, not earned or received in the course of employment hereunder, and may be retained by Physician and not turned over to JORDAN.

8. QUALIFICATIONS OF PHYSICIAN:

8.1 Physician providing services pursuant to this Agreement shall:

(a) Be Board Certified/Board Eligible;

(a.1) Physician is expected to achieve board certification within seven (7) years of completion training. Failure to achieve board certification may affect the terms of the contract.

(b) Apply for and maintain clinical privileges to practice medicine in Arizona commensurate with the procedures they will be performing pursuant to this agreement in accordance with JORDAN;

(c) Comply with the By-Laws, rules and regulations, policies and directives of JORDAN and its Medical Staff;

(d) Provide all medical services on behalf of JORDAN, which Physician is qualified to perform, in such a fashion as to meet or exceed the national, state and local standards for Arizona to the extent allowed by the facilities and equipment available at JORDAN.

9. FULL COMPLIANCE/MAINTENANCE OF LICENSE:

9.1     Physician agrees to comply with all applicable laws of the State of Arizona and the United States of America Medical Codes and Census of Ethics, and governmental rules and regulations pertaining to medical practice;

9.2     Physician at all times shall be qualified, professionally competent and duly licensed to practice medicine by the state of Arizona.

10. FACILITIES AND EQUIPMENT:

10.1    JORDAN shall provide such facilities, supplies, equipment and non-physician personnel required for the provision of Physician's services that JORDAN deems adequate to its in-patient and outpatient needs. Non-physician personnel will be recruited by and be subject to the personnel policies of JORDAN, Physician shall be consulted from time to time concerning equipment and supply needs.

11. ASSIGNABILITY:

11.1    This Agreement may be assigned by JORDAN to a subsidiary or Successor Corporation upon written notice to Physician and such assignee shall be considered the employer for purposes of this Agreement. This Agreement shall be binding upon and inure to the benefit to such assignee.

12. RELATIONSHIP BETWEEN THE PARTIES:

12.1 Employee:

During the term of this Agreement, the Physician will be engaged as a employee of JORDAN and expected to be available during the above mentioned working hours and at other times when Physician's professional advice or counsel is required.

(a) Physician shall not engage or provide professional services competitive to JORDAN, other than as provided for in this Agreement unless mutually consented to by the parties hereto.

13. TERMINATION:

13.1 This Agreement, and the terms hereof, shall continue until terminated as provided in this Section 13, or in Section 3.1.

13.2 Notwithstanding anything herein contained to the contrary, in the event that JORDAN should discontinue operating its business, or shall lose its ability to continue its operations, then this Agreement shall terminate as of the day on which JORDAN ceases operating.

13.3 In the event that Physician: a) violates any of the material conditions of this Agreement or any of the reasonable rules and regulations of JORDAN; b) loses staff privileges at any hospital at which Physician holds privileges, or otherwise has admitting privileges limited or subject to conditions not applicable at the effective date of this Agreement; c) is for any reason suspended from the practice of medicine; d) is sanctioned so as to affect materially the Physician's ability to provide medical care; e) is found guilty of criminal or professional misconduct; or f) is excluded or suspended from the Medicare, Medicaid or other state health programs, such conduct of Physician or the action of the court or regulatory agency shall constitute a breach of this Agreement by Physician and this Agreement shall terminate immediately at the sole option of JORDAN.

13.4    This Agreement shall terminate upon the death or physical or mental disability, as defined by the By-Laws, rules and regulations, policies and directives of JORDAN and its Medical Staff, of Physician which in the case of disability, prevents Physician from performing the duties hereunder.

13.5    In the event this Agreement is terminated for any of the foregoing reasons, Physician shall only be entitled to compensation and associated benefits for the time actually worked and shall not be entitled to any other damages.

14.    CONFIDENTIALITY:

14.1    Physician may have access to and obtain certain information regarding the patients, trade secrets, and statistical and unique operational and marketing data of JORDAN during the term of employment that could be valuable to other parties and injurious to JORDAN if released. Physician agrees to keep all such information confidential and not to divulge any such information to any third party for the term of this Agreement and thereafter following the termination of this Agreement.

15. CO-TERMINUS PRIVILEGES:

15.1 Notwithstanding any provisions of the By-laws, rules and regulations, and policies of JORDAN and of the Medical Staff, the Medical Staff membership and clinical privileges of the Physician shall terminate simultaneously with the termination of this Agreement. Provisions of said By-laws, rules and regulations, and policies of JORDAN and of the Medical Staff with respect to hearings, appellate review, etc., shall not apply.

16. ANNUAL REVIEW OF AGREEMENT:

16.1 The terms and provisions of this Agreement shall be reviewed annually by the executive management of JORDAN and the Physician. The purpose of this annual review is to ensure that the terms of the Agreement are being fulfilled, and are still appropriate in light of the then current financial, professional, legal and regulatory environment.

17. RENEWALS, MODIFICATION, AMENDMENTS:

17.1 No waiver or modification of this Agreement or of any covenant, condition or limitation contained herein shall be valid unless in writing and duly executed by both parties.

18. ENTIRE AGREEMENT:

18.1 This written Agreement contains the entire agreement between the parties and supersedes any and all other agreements between the parties.

19. SEVERANCE:

19.1 All agreements and covenants contained herein are severable and in the event any of them shall be held to be invalid by any competent court, this Agreement shall be interpreted as if such invalid agreement or covenant were not contained herein.

20. ARIZONA LAW CONTROLS:

20.1 This Agreement and performance hereunder shall be construed and enforceable in accordance with and pursuant to the laws of the State of Arizona.

21. BINDING EFFECT:

21.1 This Agreement shall bind and inure to the benefit of both parties and their respective successors, estates and personal representatives, but only to the extent permitted by law.

IN WITNESS WHEREOF, the parties have hereunder set their hands and seal the day and year first above written.

ATTEST:        Jordan Health Care, Inc.

               By:

               _____

               Executive Director

ATTEST:        John Doe, MD

               By:

               _____

               PHYSICIAN

**FIGURE 12-2.** Contract of Employment.

# APPENDIX A

## QUALIFICATIONS AND DUTIES OF STAFF MEMBERSHIP

<u>General Description</u>

A member of the Active Staff shall be a physician licensed to practice in the State of Arizona and who is permitted by the laws and regulations of the State of Arizona and by the Health Facility to provide patient care services on the Health Facility. Appointment to and membership on the staff shall confer on the staff member only such clinical privileges and prerogatives as have been granted by JORDAN, and shall include staff category and Department and/or Division assignments.

<u>Basic Responsibilities</u>

A.  Each member of the staff shall:

 1. Provide her/his patients with care of the generally recognized professional level of quality and efficiency;

 2. Abide by JORDAN rules and regulations, and by all other established standards, policies, rules and bylaws of the Health Facility;

 3. Discharge such staff, Department, Division, committee and Health Facility functions for which he/she is responsible by appointment, election or otherwise;

4. Prepare and complete promptly, in the prescribed manner, the medical and other required records for all patients he/she admits, or any way provides care to in the Health Facility;

5. Abide by the ethical principles of her/his profession and discipline. To refrain from fee splitting or other inducements relating to patient referral; provide for continuous care of her/his patients, refrain from delegating the responsibility for diagnosis or care of hospitalized patients to a practitioner who is not qualified to undertake this responsibility and who is not adequately supervised; seek consultation whenever necessary; and refrain from providing surgical or medical services when not physically present except under emergency circumstances;

6. Promptly notify the ED of revocation, restriction, suspension, curtailment or surrender of her/his professional license by any state, or of her/his revocation, restriction, suspension or curtailment of staff membership or privileges at any hospital or other health care institution, or the filing of charges, by the Arizona Department of Health or any law enforcement agency or health regulatory agency of the United States, or of a suit and or claim against the practitioner alleging professional liability, or any formal proceeding before any third party provider or State agency, board or society, or any change in provider status;

7. Provide services to Medical Assistance patients and other patients with personal physicians in accordance with the protocol adopted by the staff delineating responsibility for services to such patients;

8. Participate in educational programs conducted and/or sponsored by the staff and/or Health Facility;

9. Inform her/his patients of the name and function of any Medical Staff member, other than herself/himself, providing health care services to the patient.

# APPENDIX B

DUTIES OF PHYSICIAN

## GENERAL DESCRIPTION

The Physician employed at JORDAN shall be a licensed physician, board certified/board eligible by the appropriate recognized specialty board. The Physician shall have documented clinical skills, a commitment to quality patient care, medical education and shall have the ability to work harmoniously with the Medical and Nursing Staff.

## PRIMARY FUNCTION

The primary clinical duties of the Physician shall be to provide professional medical care to the patients at JORDAN.

The Physician may be engaged in other clinical duties as may be approved by appropriate Health Facility administrative authorities and are deemed in the best interest of JORDAN.

## MAJOR DUTIES

Responsible for the plan of care for each JORDAN patient with the assistance of the other Medical Staff.

Staff (3) 12 hour clinical sessions weekly.

Upholds the philosophy and mission of the Health Facility within the Department/Division.

Participates in Medical Staff meetings as required.

Provides, on a timely basis, all reports, documents and statistics as required by the Health Facility, Medical Staff, third parties and governmental agencies.

Performs all other related duties deemed necessary and appropriate in the delivery of good patient care and/or in the overall best interests of the Department/Division.

REPORTING FUNCTIONS

For administrative clinical functions, normal reporting as defined by Health Facility policy shall be directed to the Medical Director and the ED.

# APPENDIX C

THIRD PARTY BILLING ACKNOWLEDGEMENT

The Agreement dated <u>May 3rd 2004</u> by and between Physician and for the provision of professional medical services.

I acknowledge that JORDAN shall bill and collect for all professional fees for services rendered by me in connection with the above Agreement.

By:

_____

Date:

_____

# Licensure Board

The information that is contained in these two documents is enough to get you started on both applications. Prior to the submission of the waiver application to the Department of Health, the physician has to be licensed in your state to practice medicine. The fact that the physician has graduated from medical school does not automatically allow the doctor to practice medicine. The licensure board has to now evaluate their education to ensure that all of the requirements for a state license have been satisfactorily met. Also, there are several national examinations that have to be taken and passed by the doctor. As well, the medical school of attendance should be listed in the International Medical Education Directory (IMED) and be a graduate of a medical school listed in the World Health Organization (WHO) World Directory of Medical Schools.

Most physicians are well aware of these requirements, and many of them already have Educational Commission for Foreign Medical Graduates (ECFMG) Certification. Yet, on occasion a physician will be informed that he has not met an educational prerequisite required by a certain state due to the denunciation of one, or more foreign academic courses. The initial notification of this circumstance is often quite heart wrenching and emotional. Unfortunately, the bottom line is that if the physician fails to obtain a license, the application cannot go forward. However, the ECFMG has vast resources available to assist in the process. During the licensure process the physician may need a letter of support to go along with the application, which you can write using similar wording as indicated in figure 12-3. It would also be a good idea to have one or more of your board members write a letter of support as well.

## Sample Physician Support letter

May 15, 2004

John Smith, Asst. Exec. Director

State of Kentucky

Division of Consumer Affairs

State Board of Medical Examiners

140 West Front Street, 5th Floor

Louisville, KY 80578

Re: John Doe, MD

Please accept this correspondence as a letter of support for this physician. He is committed to working in a medically underserved and health profession shortage area. Dr. Doe has many references from Louisville Medical Center, which is a major teaching hospital.

This physician is community oriented, and has expressed a strong desire to help those residents living in an urban community. His instructors have indicated that he is bright, hardworking and treats his patients with respect. He has also received an award honoring him for outstanding performance in an outpatient setting, and for his clinical research on the improvement of testing for ocular cancer in the community from Roosevelt College. Should you have any further questions please feel free to give me a call at (123) 456-7890.

Sincerely,

Executive Director

**FIGURE 12-3.** Support letter for licensure.

# Country Of Expatriate Origin

This detail along with any other specific information requests should be presented to your state along with an attestation from the physician indicating that their country is not expected them to return upon completion of their education. This is important, as there are some countries that have indicated to these doctors that they are required to return back to their country of origin for various reasons. You can use the format in figure 12-4 to generate the letter and figure 12-5 to notarize the attestation.

### Sample Return of Expatriate Letter

May 31, 2004

State of New York
Department of Health and Senior Services
Division of Family Health Services
Albany, NY 04785

I, John Doe, MD residing at 101 Your Town Road, Manhattan, New York do hereby certify that there are no provisions for my return to my home country Canada upon completion of my medical residency at Columbia Medical College located in Brooklyn, New York.

Additionally, no contract exists between the Canadian Government and me as a J-1 VISA Waiver applicant.

Signed,
John Doe, MD

**FIGURE 12-4.** Waiver Letter.

STATE OF NEW YORK
COUNTY OF GEORGIA

Personally appeared before me, the undersigned authority in and for the said county and state, on this <u>31st</u> day of <u>May,</u> <u>2004</u>, within my jurisdiction, the within named <u>John Doe, MD</u>, who acknowledges that he/she executed the above and foregoing instrument.

_____ (NOTARY PUBLIC)

My commission expires:

**FIGURE 12-5.** Notary of Attestation Letter.

# Needs Analysis

In the interim while you are waiting on the medical license to be approved, the next step in the process is to put together a needs analysis that can be submitted to your state Department of Health for its approval on the waiver application. The Department of Health's approval of this wavier is required by the INS. So it is tantamount that you make a compelling case that the community needs this physician and cannot hire an American doctor for various reasons. And, these barriers can range from an inability to recruit a specific specialty to a complete shortage of willing and able physicians of any discipline who would work in your specific geographic area.

## Census Track

How do you build your case? The Federal government publishes data on every neighborhood in America. The data is a compilation of economic and social indicators that map specific provider ratios to population needs. For instance, if you look up the zip code 80856 on the report, it may indicate that geographically those citizens residing within the census tracts (59-62, 33, 18 and 20) have been designated by the federal government as residing in a "Health Professional Shortage Area." For that reason, the census track that you are located in seems to be in need of doctors. But, there is a lot more information that will need to be put into a comprehensive analysis. The package that you submit is going to have to identify all of the current providers in the area, and it has to elaborate on the reasons as to why they cannot service this same population. In reality, many organizations hire a consultant to put together their needs analysis. Yet, in order to cut down considerably on costs you can do the bulk of the research and then subsequently work in tandem with the consultant.

## Timetable

A well-polished and wide-ranging study should fully address each concern that your Department of Health will readily outline for you prior to submission of your request. In fact, you should contact someone in that office and ask for assistance in submitting a waiver application. Just keep in mind that they probably receive a great deal of these requests, and may not have the experienced personnel and resources available to accommodate your particular timetable. The analysis in figure 12-6 is designed to substantiate the need to obtain a waiver for an Internal Medicine physician.

## Sample Waiver Needs Analysis

### Description and Unmet Need

HAMILTON Health Care is a not-for-profit community based organization that is licensed as an ambulatory care facility by the Texas Department of Health and Senior Services for the provision of both drug abuse treatment and primary care services. We are the only Texas licensed ambulatory facility in Houston and Penny County that is designed to be a complete "one stop shop" or integrated healthcare delivery system for substance abuse and primary care. There are only two-licensed mental health and drug treatment facilities in Houston. They are HAMILTON Health Care and DIAMOND Health Care. DIAMOND is strictly a methadone center and does not provide any primary care services.

However, we are unique in that we have put together a comprehensive program as suggested by the United States Department of Health and Human Services, Centers for Disease Control and Prevention (CDC), Center for Substance Abuse Treatment (CSAT) and National Institute on Drug Abuse (NIDA).

HAMILTON, the only primary health-care facility serving minorities in the area, prides itself on providing access to quality, community-based health delivery with a holistic approach (emphasizing the importance of one's total wellness by serving their interdependent needs), "Looking at the World through HAMILTON", Americana Medical Associates and National Corporation, August 1962, p.27.

HAMILTON Health Care began servicing the community in Houston in 1977. Our primary focus is to provide both drug, alcohol and primary care services. As time grew, a much more disturbing trend appeared as we interviewed hundreds of men and women afflicted with life-shattering addictions. Our client base is 16,000 and each of those individuals come into our facility at least three times a week for a total of 26,000 contacts per year. During this time we are finding that the majority of the people who came to us for substance abuse counseling and treatment suffer from numerous health problems.

These problems ranged from AIDS, to hepatitis, congenital syphilis, TB and parents reporting low-birth weight babies as a result of their drug use. In accordance with the United Counties Department of Health and Human Services 1976 report, "United Counties and Healthy People 1975 Review", we saw first-hand that the very young, older adults, and members of minority groups were at an increased risk for many infectious diseases. Mothers were reporting that as a direct result of their drug use, their babies were being born prematurely, and had to be detoxified soon after delivery for drugs such as cocaine and heroin.

As we began to provide services, we found that the neonatal mortality rate and the number of post neonatal deaths showed no, or very little improvement for minorities over the last ten (10) years.

Records also indicated that when it came to obtaining prenatal care, minority women had less of a chance to receive care than white females.

The health problems that we encounter include hypertension, low birth weight babies, high infant mortality rates, lack of proper immunization, diabetes, heart disease, cervical cancer, prostate cancer, kidney disease, sexually transmitted diseases, AIDS (a recent report indicates that Texas has the highest incidence of AIDS of any city in the United States), poor nutrition, drug, alcohol and tobacco addictions and abuse and tuberculosis.

As a direct result of providing hundreds of referrals for internal medicine we began to observe that when people were referred to various institutional healthcare providers they would not make the appointments. The major consensus was that these institutions were not user friendly and there was a lack of concern for the dignity of the patient. And, most importantly, statistics prove that minorities do not seek healthcare outside their neighborhoods.

In addition to those preventable health problems that traditionally beset minorities, state health statistics disclose these alarming facts:

- ✓ The low birth weight infants rate in Texas is 11.3%, compared to 6.8% statewide;
- ✓ The infant mortality rate in Texas is 14.3%, compared to 9.2% statewide;

- ✓ The infant mortality rate among Blacks in Texas is 19.5% and 13.7% among Hispanics;
- ✓ The immunization rate in Texas is only 60%;
- ✓ Texas has the highest number of reported AIDS/HIV cases of any U.S. city;
- ✓ Two-thirds of all AIDS cases in Texas are directly attributable to IV drug use;
- ✓ It's estimated that 1 of every 10 Texas newborns may be exposed to drug use during pregnancy.

Our experience is that once a patient is in our facility and we can provide both Substance Abuse Counseling and Health Services on the spot, the chances of a patient missing or foregoing treatment are substantially decreased. By implementing this form of integrated treatment, the patient has all the available resources on hand and on demand. This treatment delivery system has positively impacted the health care of men, women and children in the community. This is especially critical when it pertains to young children. Compared to preschoolers from more affluent areas, young children living in poor neighborhoods are several times more likely to be hospitalized with conditions avoidable with adequate ambulatory care.

In our service area many communicable diseases especially sexually transmitted diseases, tuberculosis, and HIV infection are increasing at alarming rates, even among patients in treatment for alcohol and other drug abuse. The screening prevention, and control of infectious disease has become a critically important function for alcohol and other drug abuse treatment programs, both to protect our patients and staff who work with them. Injection drug users because of their high-risk behaviors and physical susceptibility are particularly vulnerable to acquired immunodeficiency syndrome (AIDS) and other diseases, most notably tuberculosis (TB) and sexually transmitted diseases (STDs). In 1977, nearly one in three (29 percent) of new AIDS cases occurred among men who use intravenous drugs.

Additionally, in 1977 the number of AIDS cases among women jumped by nearly 10 percent, compared with nearly 2.5 percent increase among men. Slightly over half of those women were infected through heterosexual intercourse, with 6 of 10 women having had male partners who were intravenous drug users. Nearly half of the women with new AIDS cases became infected through their own injection drug use. Women also account for about half of all sexually transmitted infections that occur each year. The transmission of an STD to an unborn child or during childbirth can have devastating effects on the baby.

For patients seen in a drug treatment program, addiction is often associated with a host of ills, such as poverty, homelessness, deprivation, unemployment and violence. These patients frequently lack access to primary health care, and often have little or no medical care before they enter drug treatment. Alcohol and other drug treatment providers, who work with and understand these patients, are ideally situated to reach out and provide the services these patients desperately need. They should perform these medical services on-site as infectious diseases are so prevalent among drug users.

Individuals who are dependent on drugs are represented inconsistently in the population with human immunodeficiency virus (HIV) and AIDS; tuberculosis; syphilis; and hepatitis B and C. Patients who enter drug treatment programs are at risk of having one or more of these diseases. For example, there has been a steady increase in the incidence of hepatitis B, despite the availability of a vaccine since 1972. Most of the increase is attributed to injection drug use. The prevalence of hepatitis C in injection drug users is also high (Anyone, U.PK., Any Journal of Epidemiology 1234:5678-9, 1977).

Additionally, injection drug use is closely linked to the spread of HIV. Patients infected with HIV, because of their impaired immune systems, are at increased risk of developing numerous infections, the majority of which represent reactivation of prior infection. However, HIV-infected persons are far more likely to develop active TB after exposure to TB than HIV-negative persons. An increase in cases of tuberculoses appears to be related to HIV infection and is seen primarily in the 25 to 44 age group. Multi drug-resistant tuberculosis has been detected in a growing number of states and is seen especially in large cities with high rates of drug use, homelessness, and HIV infection.

Further, the association between syphilis and drug use has been substantiated by retrospective studies and is particularly strong among cocaine users (Anybody, H.W., Journal of Serious Diseases 987:654-321,1970).

Persons enrolled in drug treatment programs are vulnerable to a wide range of debilitating diseases such as Endocarditis which occurs primarily in persons who inject drugs; Bacterium/septicemia which is a bacterial invasion of the blood stream that results from use or sharing contaminated needles and other drug paraphernalia; Fungal infections-such infections, including candidiasis and histoplasmosis, which can be relatively harmless in patients with normal immune systems can be life threatening in patients with compromised immune systems such as those with HIV; Body lice/scabies and venereal warts.

Many drug users are reluctant to become involved with traditional medical providers because of previous poor treatment and insensitive care. As a result, they may not seek testing for and treatment of infectious diseases. In addition, lack of access to health care, either because of financial or other socioeconomic reasons, may mean that drug users may have had minimal or no medical care before enrolling in a drug treatment program. Drug treatment providers are ideally positioned to reach out to their populations and provide medical services and infectious disease screening.

All patients in treatment should have access to therapeutic medical services. Due to the fact that drug use can place patients at increased risk for infectious diseases, the Centers for Disease Control and Prevention (CDC) recommends that treatment programs screen all patients for TB and all injection users for HIV. Upon entering treatment and periodically thereafter, patients should receive an assessment, physical examination, serologic and other laboratory screening, TB screening, counseling and follow-up medical care as appropriate.

Drug treatment centers offer the best opportunities to approach and intervene with the substance-using woman when she is pregnant. The child's birth may give her a powerful motive to seek treatment for addiction. Early intervention efforts during the prenatal period increase the likelihood that she will successfully recover from alcohol and other drug abuse.

It is equally important to provide the pregnant, substance-using women with optimal, comprehensive obstetrical care. The results of prenatal drug exposure are well documented and can include intrauterine growth retardation, premature and low birth weight, central nervous system damage, and congenital physical malformations, among others.

A continuum of follow-up services is a third critical element for an improved quality of life for the substance-using woman and her family. She often lives in a stressful environment that may include physical and sexual abuse, single parenthood, and limited financial and social support. Interventions during the postnatal period are needed to help her successfully parent her child and abstain from the use of alcohol and other drugs.

**Figure 12-6**. Needs Analysis to Support Waiver.

## State Approves

Once the state approves the medical license and grants the waiver this information will be forwarded to the doctor's immigration attorney. At this point the attorney will submit the request for the visa along with supporting documents to the INS for subsequent approval. This process can take several weeks, and if the physician's current visa expires there are steps that the attorney can take to ensure that the doctor has a current visa in place.

# Chapter 13
# Psychotherapy and Counseling

The guidelines by which you will run your organization must be built upon a strong policy and procedure structure. This structure is visible both internally and externally. Fundamentally, the internal policy is designed to run your agency on a day-to-day basis. This policy will control important functions such as hiring, compensation, training and terminating employees. There should also be procedures for granting vacations and allocating days off.

## Path of Responsibility

On the other hand, your polices and procedures are viewed externally to ensure compliance with many grant and regulatory agency requirements such as affirmative action, sexual harassment, HIPPA and the Family Medical Leave Act. These procedures are not optional. It is your responsibility as a director to ensure that everyone in the organization follows each and every rule. The organizational management structure should also be outlined in full detail. The purpose is to visibly provide a key to the path of responsibility for a given function within the company. The policies and procedures that are contained in figures 13-1 and 13-2 are complete and have been designed to apply to a psychotherapy/counseling setting, psychotherapy with primary care setting, or the integrated behavioral healthcare setting. The integrated setting is comprised of primary care and psychotherapy with pharmacotherapy. However, the integrated setting requires an additional set of more sophisticated operating procedures, which are included in the chapter regarding pharmacotherapy. The manual is divided into several key segments for a total of 32 sections in all. Also, each section is listed in summary and then in full detail. Yet, most importantly, your Board of Directors must approve all the sections that are eventually adopted into your organization. Moreover, the board must authorize any subsequent changes, as well.

## Sample Policy and Procedures Detail

*Section 1A:* CONFIDENTIALITY

Today's healthcare industry is extremely competitive. To that end, HAMILTON is committed to building a strong organizational environment in which we can grow and flourish. The healthcare environment has become increasingly contentious. Rivals are constantly attempting to either consolidate or take over individual and group practices, as well as, independent clinics. To that end, it is our policy to maintain all company operating information on a need to know basis, particularly patient information as per HIPPA guidelines. All operational information obtained while in your employ here at HAMILTON is <u>confidential</u>. This information includes computer operating systems, patient statistics, procedural systems and any information regarding HAMILTON's internal operating systems. Furthermore, this information is <u>not</u> to be <u>distributed, copied</u> or <u>disseminated</u> in any manner without the express consent of the Executive Director, Chief Operating Officer or a member of the Board of Directors. Any deviation to this policy will result in <u>immediate termination</u> and <u>possible litigation</u>. It is HAMILTON's policy to prosecute to the fullest extent of the law possible for any damages inflicted upon this organization by information released or distributed without proper authorization.

*Section 1B:* STATEMENT OF PURPOSE

This Section describes the policy and procedures for the development and use of the Manual.

Section 2: STRUCTURE OF THE PERSONNEL PROGRAM

Policies and procedures describing the Personnel Program including the responsibilities of HAMILTON's Board of Directors, Executive Director and the Chief Operating Officer.

*Section 3:* AFFIRMATIVE ACTION

This Section includes a statement of compliance with Title VII of the Civil Rights Act of 1964 and the Equal Employment Act of 1972 and the New Jersey Law Against Discrimination or N.J.S.A. 10:5, et seq. The Section outlines the actions HAMILTON, will take to ensure non-discrimination throughout the organization.

*Section 4:* SEXUAL HARASSMENT

This Section defines sexual harassment and the steps HAMILTON will take to ensure that it does not occur.

*Section 5:* PERSONNEL RECORDS

Policy and procedures describing what information will be kept in personnel files and who will have access to them.

*Section 6:* EMPLOYEE SELECTION PROCESS

Policy and procedures describing employee selection, including the completion and screening of applications, interview procedures and final selection.

*Section 7:* EMPLOYEE STATUS

Policy and procedures describing probationary, permanent, hourly and contract employee status. The Section also defines the status of graduate student workers, volunteers and interns.

*Section 8:* PERFORMANCE EVALUATIONS

Policy and procedures describing performance evaluations and the manner in which they will be conducted.

*Section 9:* CLASSIFICATION PLAN

This Section describes how positions within HAMILTON will be classified.

*Section 10:* COMPENSATION PLAN

This policy describes compensation for classified positions and adjustments for comparable positions in New Jersey.

*Section 11:* PAY PERIODS

Policy and procedures describing how employees will be paid, what deductions will be made and how payment will be provided.

*Section 12:* SALARIES AND WAGES

Policy and procedures describing eligibility for compensation and how increases will be awarded.

*Section 13:* FRINGE BENEFITS

Policy and procedures describing fringe benefits available to HAMILTON employees.

*Section 14:* VACATION LEAVE

Policy and procedures describing how vacation time is accrued, as well as how it is approved, used and paid.

*Section 15:* SICK LEAVE

Policy and procedures describing how sick leave is accrued and how it may be used.

*Section 16:* PERSONAL LEAVE

Policy and procedures describing how personal leave is accrued and how it may be used.

*Section 17:* HOLIDAYS

Policy and procedures describing the observance of holidays at HAMILTON.

*Section 18:* LEAVES OF ABSENCE

Policy and procedures describing leaves of absence categories and all of the conditions that apply to each.

*Section 19:* CAREER DEVELOPMENT

Policy and procedures describing career development activities, hours available to employees, and the guidelines for reimbursement.

*Section 20:* REIMBURSEMENT FOR TRAVEL

Policy and procedures governing reimbursement for employee travel and expense.

*Section 21:* **EMPLOYEE GRIEVANCES**

Policy and procedures describing how to file a grievance, who will hear it, and the time limits for response.

*Section 22:* **DISCIPLINARY ACTIONS**

Policy and procedures describing violations of HAMILTON policies and corrective actions to be taken.

*Section 23:* **SUSPENSION**

Policy and procedures describing the causes for suspension and the manner in which it may be implemented.

*Section 24:* **DEMOTION**

Policy and procedures describing the causes for demotion and the manner in which it may be implemented.

*Section 25:* **TERMINATION**

Policy and procedures describing types of termination, notices and payments provided, as well as exit procedures.

*Section 26:* **NEPOTISM**

Policy statement regarding the recruitment and employment of immediate family members of HAMILTON employees.

*Section 27:* **CONFLICT OF INTEREST**

This Section provides the guidelines in which HAMILTON will follow to guard against conflict of interest.

*Section 28:* SAFETY AND ACCIDENT PREVENTION

Policy and procedures for ensuring a safe working environment and how to report accidents and employee responsibilities.

*Section 29*: EMPLOYEE ASSISTANCE

Policy and procedures describing the assistance HAMILTON will provide to troubled employees.

*Section 30:* EMPLOYEE SUGGESTIONS AND COMMENTS

Procedures for making recommendations and changes to operations.

*Section 31:* DRUG TESTING

Official corporate substance abuse policy regarding HAMILTON's commitment to a drug free workplace.

*Section 32:* SECURITY

Policy statement outlining personnel and property safety.

**FIGURE 13-1**. Counseling Policy and Procedures Index.

## Section 1 - STATEMENT OF PURPOSE

Definition: Personnel policies and procedures are guidelines and rules established by HAMILTON's Board of Directors to (a) provide staff with a systematic approach to HAMILTON's functions, and (b) create efficiency and order, and (c) provide a process for facilitating grievances and complaints.

Policy: HAMILTON shall develop, maintain and update personnel policies and procedures.

Procedures: 1.1 The Board of Directors shall commission the Chief Operating Officer to develop personnel policies and procedures.

1.2 The Board of Directors shall adopt policies and procedures designed to ensure compliance with its wishes and intentions.

1.3 The Board shall require an annual update of personnel policies and procedures.

1.4 Policies and procedures developed, changed or deleted by the Chief Operating Officer require full approval of the Board of Directors.

1.5 Policies and procedures shall be updated at the time of adoption or revision.

## Section 2 - STRUCTURE OF THE PERSONNEL PROGRAM

Definition: The Personnel Program consists of the methods by which HAMILTON establishes personnel policies and procedures.

Policy: HAMILTON shall maintain a structured Personnel Program.

Procedures: 2.1 HAMILTON's Board of Directors shall exercise control over personnel policies and procedures through the adoption of policy statements and procedural actions.

2.2 The Chief Operating Officer shall act as Personnel Officer for HAMILTON, shall interpret and administer all policy statements adopted by the Board of Directors, and shall be vested with the authority to hire and terminate HAMILTON personnel.

2.3 The Chief Operating Officer or his/her designee shall provide each new HAMILTON employee with information concerning hours of operation, fringe benefits, and a copy of this manual. After a new employee has reviewed the manual, the Chief Operating Officer or his/her designee shall answer any questions he or she may have concerning these policies and procedures. The new employee shall sign a written statement indicating that he or she has reviewed and understood the policies and procedures. The signed statement shall be entered in the employee's personnel file within two (2) weeks of the date of hire.

2.4 During the course of employment, any individual who has questions about these policies and procedures shall contact the Chief Operating Officer for clarification in writing.

2.5 The Chief Operating Officer shall be responsible for reviewing these policies and procedures on an annual basis and for making recommendations for revisions to the Board of Directors.

2.6 Following review of recommendations provided by the Chief Operating Officer, the Board of Directors may change these policies and procedures.

2.7 Revised policies and procedures shall be circulated among HAMILTON staff by the Chief Operating Officer. Questions concerning revised policies and procedures shall be addressed to the Chief Operating Officer. Employees shall sign a distribution sheet indicating review of revised policies and procedures.

2.8 These policies and procedures shall be enforced consistently for all programs sponsored by HAMILTON.

2.9 If a new program requires revising of these policies and procedures, the Chief Operating Officer may make recommendations for revision to the Board of Directors. The rationale for each revision should be included in the recommendations.

## Section 3 - AFFIRMATIVE ACTION

Definition: Affirmative Action is a set of procedures designed to ensure that an organization is free of discriminatory practices.

Policy: This Section is based upon the following practices:

1. HAMILTON shall recruit, hire, utilize, train and promote for all job classifications without regard to age, sex, marital status, handicap, race, ancestry, color, national origin, or political affiliations.

2. HAMILTON shall make decisions concerning selection, utilization, training, promotion, program services and operations in a manner that shall further the principles of equal employment opportunity and affirmative action.

3. HAMILTON shall make decisions concerning compensation, benefits, leaves of absence and career development in a manner that shall further the principles of equal opportunity and affirmative action.

4. HAMILTON shall create and maintain a working environment that is free from discrimination and harassment of all employees.

5. HAMILTON shall assure that reasonable accommodations are provided for the physical and mental limitations of applicants and employees.

Procedures: 3.1 A personnel manual, including Affirmative Action policies and procedures, shall be prepared by the Chief Operating Officer for approval by the Board of Directors.

3.2 All qualified applicants shall be given equal consideration for employment, and the Chief Operating Officer shall consider applicants according to merit, without regard for race, creed, color, national origin, age, sex, handicap or religious or political affiliation.

3.3 Job interviews shall be structured to avoid inquiry into irrelevant areas of an applicant's personal situation, (i.e., questions relating to child care arrangements, spouse's occupation, religious views etc.)

3.4 The Chief Operating Officer shall provide an effective employee performance evaluation program based upon job-related performance requirements and organizational goals. The program shall be administered in a manner that prohibits judgments about character and personality traits.

3.5 The Chief Operating Officer or his/her designees shall conduct an annual review of HAMILTON classification plan to ensure that qualification requirements are realistic, valid and representative of the minimum education, training and experience essential to successfully fill a position.

3.6 The Chief Operating Officer shall provide an effective grievance and appeal system so that complaints alleging discrimination can be fully investigated and so that corrective actions can be taken when necessary.

3.7  The Chief Operating Officer or his/her designee shall administer a written exit interview program to identify and resolve problems in employee turnover.

## Section 4 - SEXUAL HARASSMENT

Definition: Sexual harassment includes repeated, offensive sexual flirtations, advances, propositions, continual or repeated verbal commentaries about an individuals' body, sexually degrading words used to describe an individual and the display in the workplace of sexually suggestive objects or pictures. Harassment may be verbal, physical or visual and may occur among co-workers as well as supervisors and subordinates.

Policy: This Section is based upon the following policies:

1. HAMILTON believes that employers have an obligation to keep the workplace free from sexual harassment. In order to do so, we will investigate situations whenever we are advised of a problem or observe what we consider to be a problem.

2. An employee's rejection of sexual advances does not have to result in the loss of tangible job benefits to constitute a valid and actionable complaint.

3. HAMILTON shall prohibit harassment of its employees in any form and such conduct may result in disciplinary action up to and including dismissal.

4. Supervisory conduct must be free of any behavior that may be considered discriminatory or harassing or any actions, which may be interpreted as being taken for personal gain or advantage.

5. The Chief Operating Officer and supervisors shall be observant of the potential for harassment in their areas or departments.

6. The Chief Operating Officer and supervisors shall create a climate that is receptive to complaints.

7. All discussions concerning complaints shall be held in the strictest of confidence.

Procedures: 4.1 Upon learning of a case of potential harassment, a supervisor shall acknowledge it immediately and shall report it to the Chief Operating Officer on the same day, or as soon as possible.

4.2 The Chief Operating Officer shall discuss any concerns with an employee who feels that he or she is the victim of discrimination. If possible, the complaint shall be resolved at that time.

4.3 If an employee is not satisfied with the results of a discussion with the Chief Operating Officer, he or she may utilize the formal grievance procedures outlined in Section 20 of the policies and procedures.

## Section 5 - PERSONNEL RECORDS

Definition: Personnel records consist of documents and materials relating to an employee's qualifications, status and performance.

Policy: HAMILTON shall maintain complete personnel files for each of its employees.

Procedures: 5.1 The Operations Manager shall be responsible for maintaining personnel files. These files shall be considered official records and all pertinent information received by supervisors concerning employees should be forwarded to the Operations Manager for inclusion in files.

5.2 An employee may submit materials for inclusion in his or her personnel file at any time while employed by HAMILTON. Such materials should be forwarded to the Operations Manager.

5.3 An employee may examine his or her personnel file in the office of the Chief Operating Officer during business hours. The Operations Manager shall be present when an employee examines the contents of his or her file.

5.4 Employee personnel records shall be considered confidential and shall be accessible only to the following individuals:

a.　　the employee concerned;

b. the Chief Operating Officer, Executive Director, Clinic Director, Operations Manager, Board Treasurer, and Board Secretary of HAMILTON;

c. the legal representative of the employee if there is pending litigation and only with the consent of the employee.

5.5 All personnel records shall include the following items:

a. application for employment and/or resume;

b. signed offer of employment letter;

c. job description(s) for position(s) held by the staff member;

d. copies of degrees, certificates or licenses, if mandatory for the position(s) that the employee holds;

e. current address of the employee;

f. signed statement indicating review of HAMILTON personnel policies and procedures manual;

g. insurance and tax forms;

h. performance evaluations;

i. documentation of disciplinary actions;

j. changes in employee status and salary, if any;

k. documentation of leaves of absence, if any;

l. career development information, and;

m. other documents relevant to the employee, including materials submitted by the employee for inclusion in his or her record;

n. confidentiality statement.

5.6 Records on terminated employees will be kept in a confidential inactive file. In addition to the materials outlined in 5.5 above, these files shall include:

a. letter of resignation, if submitted;

b. record of exit interview;

c. information concerning the termination of employee's benefits, and;

d. forwarding address (if provided by the employee).

5.7 The Chief Operating Officer shall be the only HAMILTON employee with the authority to release information from active and inactive personnel records. Information released from personnel files shall be limited to:

a. name of employee;

b. starting date of employment;

c. final date of employment (if applicable);

d. other information authorized for release through the written consent of the current or former employee.

## Section 6 - EMPLOYEE SELECTION PROCESS

Definition: The selection process is the manner in which applicants are considered for positions in HAMILTON.

Policy: HAMILTON shall develop, maintain and update selection procedures.

Procedures: 6.1 Unsolicited applications for employment shall be considered for all classes and positions for which applicants qualify or request consideration.

6.2 Initial review of the candidates for an open position shall be conducted through applications and resumes. The applications and resumes shall be reviewed by the Chief Operating Officer or his/her designee who shall select the candidates to be interviewed.

6.3 HAMILTON employees who wish to apply for a vacant position must follow the same procedures as other applicants.

6.4 The Chief Operating Officer may request that supervisors and other staff members participate in applicant interviews.

6.5 The Chief Operating Officer or his/her designee shall interview no more than five (5) candidates for each vacant position.

6.6 The Chief Operating Officer may require more than one interview before a final decision is reached.

6.7    If an appropriate candidate is not identified, the Chief Operating Officer may reinstate the selection process.

6.8    Verbal notice may be provided to the successful candidate after an offer of employment letter has been signed by the Chief Operating Officer and mailed to the candidate selected.

6.9    All participants not selected shall receive written notification of HAMILTON's decision from the Chief Operating Officer or his/her designee within ten (10) calendar days of the date of selection.

6.10    HAMILTON is unable to pay travel costs for interviews or relocation costs for new employees, unless such costs are recommended by the Chief Operating Officer and approved by the Board of Directors.

6.11    The Board of Directors shall establish the selection process to be utilized to fill the position of Executive Director and Chief Operating Officer. Upon completion, said procedures shall be documented in writing and included in this Section.

## Section 7 - EMPLOYMENT STATUS

Definition: Employee status is the position an employee has obtained through length of service and performance.

Policy: HAMILTON shall designate status for each of its employees.

Procedures: 7.1 <u>Probationary Status</u>: All full-time permanent and hourly employees, whether by selection or promotion, shall be on probationary status during the first six months of employment in a position. This probationary period shall be considered as part of the process for determining the qualifications of candidates for continued employment with HAMILTON. During the probationary period, the employee may be demoted, suspended or terminated with or without cause at the sole discretion of the Chief Operating Officer.

To determine the employee's ability and other attributes, the work and conduct of the employee shall be evaluated in writing by the Chief Operating Officer or his/her designee at the completion of the six-month probationary period. An employee's probationary period may be extended by the Chief Operating Officer for a maximum of 90 days. Extension of probation must be established in writing prior to the end of the initial six-month probationary period. Written notice must include the reason for the extension and specific goals for satisfactory job performance. Extension of probation shall exclude any raise in salary.

At the conclusion of the probationary period, as extended if necessary, the Chief Operating Officer will advise the probationary employee whether he or she will become a regular employee of HAMILTON.

7.2     Permanent Full Time Status: Acquired by an employee with proper qualifications who has been placed in a budgeted position and is retained in the position after completion of the probationary period. A permanent full-time employee is one who works 40.0 hours per week and is eligible for all employee benefits (see Section 13 of these Policies and Procedures).

7.3     Hourly Employee Status: Acquired by an employee who possesses the minimum qualifications and has been placed in a position that is budgeted for less than 40.0 hours per week. Fringe benefits do not apply, unless specified in writing by the Chief Operating Officer.

7.4     Hourly Employee Status (Consultants): When HAMILTON requires specialized services which are not available from its current staff, the Chief Operating Officer may contract for these services with private persons or agencies. Performance shall be determined by the conditions of the contract. Contract employees shall not be eligible for fringe benefits.

7.5     Graduate Student Employee Status: Graduate students may be employed to assist HAMILTON and may be reimbursed on a flat rate or hourly basis. The Chief Operating Officer shall determine such rates at the time of employment. Job responsibilities and rates of reimbursement shall be specified in writing by the Chief Operating Officer. Graduate student workers shall not be eligible for fringe benefits.

7.6   <u>Student Intern Status</u>: Said interns <u>shall not</u> receive financial reimbursement from HAMILTON, nor shall they be eligible for fringe benefits. HAMILTON shall comply with university requirements for student evaluation. Interns shall work a maximum of 40.0 hours per week for no less than six weeks. Specific hours and assignments shall be determined by the Chief Operating Officer.

7.7   Employees, including graduate students, and interns shall be provided with a copy of this manual by the Chief Operating Officer and shall be subject to all the provisions thereof.

7.8 Volunteers shall go through the same screening process as new hires, as indicated in Section 6. Volunteers will not be paid, and are subject to the same policies and procedures as any other HAMILTON staff member.

## Section 8 - PERFORMANCE EVALUATION

Definition: A performance evaluation is a review of the quality and quantity of work completed by an employee. Evaluations are conducted to determine strengths and areas that need improvement, to clarify positional expectations, and to plan professional development for an employee.

Policy: HAMILTON shall complete performance evaluations for all employees.

Procedures: 8.1 During the recruitment process, the Chief Operating Officer or his/her designee shall provide each new employee with a schedule of performance evaluation dates and with written documentation of the criteria shall include, but need not be limited to, job descriptions, personnel policies and procedures and program objectives.

8.2 Every performance evaluation shall specify the date for the next scheduled evaluation and a review and update of written criteria to be utilized during the next scheduled evaluation.

8.3 In the case of the Executive Director and Chief Operating Officer, written statements of performance criteria shall be prepared by the Board of Directors at the beginning of each contract period. For all other HAMILTON employees, written performance criteria shall be prepared by the Chief Operating Officer, or his/her designee.

8.4     All employees shall receive a performance evaluation from the Chief Operating Officer, or his/her designee at the end of their probationary period and on an annual basis from the date of initial evaluation.

8.5     The Executive Director and Chief Operating Officer of HAMILTON shall be evaluated on an annual basis by the Board of Directors.

8.6     A special performance evaluation may be required when an employee's performance deviates from positional expectations. This evaluation must be designated as either a warning or commendation evaluation and is to be included in the employee's personnel file.

8.7     Performance evaluations shall be considered in determining salary increases within the limits of the compensation plan. (see Section 10 of these Policies and Procedures). In addition, performance evaluations shall be a factor in promotion, demotion, suspension, dismissal, rehiring and recommendations.

8.8     Raises may be available at the completion of annual and commendation performance evaluation. This does not mean that an employee will automatically receive a raise in salary. The Chief Operating Officer must recommend an approval for salary increment at the completion of the performance evaluation process.

8.9     Every performance evaluation shall be completed by the employee and the Chief Operating Officer or his/her designee within ten (10) consecutive working days from the evaluation due date.

8.10 Upon completion, each performance evaluation shall be signed by the Chief Operating Officer or his/her designee, and the evaluation shall be placed in the appropriate personnel file.

## Section 9 - CLASSIFICATION PLAN

Definition: The classification plan is a division of positions according to required knowledge, skills, experience and responsibilities.

Policy: HAMILTON shall develop, maintain and update a classification plan.

Procedures: 9.1 The Board of Directors shall commission the Chief Operating Officer to develop a classification plan.

9.2 The Board of Directors shall adopt such policies and procedures prepared by the Chief Operating Officer that comply with the Board's intentions and wishes.

9.3 The Board shall require an annual update of the classification plan.

9.4 The Chief Operating Officer shall establish two employee classifications: exempt and non-exempt. These classifications shall comply with the Walsh-Health Public Contracts Act and the Fair Labor Standards Act. The Acts state that jobs classified as executive, administrative and professional shall be exempt and that jobs not falling into these classifications shall be non-exempt. There will also be two categories of exempt employees, essential and non-essential exempt. The persons who fall in the category of essential exempt are as follows:

- Executive Director
- Chief Operating Officer
- Operations Manager
- Administrative Director
- Financial Manager
- Security Director
- Medical Director
- Clinic Director
- Administrative Assistants
- Clinical Coordinators
- Nursing Director

9.5     Employees in non-exempt classifications shall be eligible for compensation time (equal time off) or for overtime reimbursement for any time in excess of 40.0 hours in a calendar week. Employees in exempt classifications shall not be eligible for compensation time or overtime reimbursement; however, essential exempt employees will be eligible for administrative compensation time.

9.6     The classification plan shall assign each position in HAMILTON to an appropriate class. Assignment to classes shall be made on the basis of knowledge, skills, experience and responsibilities required for a position. A class may include more than one position.

9.7     Positions in a single class shall be sufficiently alike to permit:

a)      requirements for similar levels of experience and education,

b) application of the same pay range. Each position in a single class shall have:

(1) a concise, descriptive title;

(2) a statement of necessary qualifications, and;

(3) a description of the duties and responsibilities required by the position.

9.8 The Chief Operating Officer may review the duties and responsibilities of positions and recommend the creation of new positions and/or elimination of existing positions from the classification plan. Recommendations shall be made to the Board of Directors.

9.9 The Chief Operating Officer may, upon his or her own initiative, or upon the recommendation of a supervisor, reassign a position to a different class. Reassignment may be made when the duties required for a position change and the reassignment can be accomplished within budget limitations.

9.10 Job descriptions shall take into consideration the requirements of the job and shall be descriptive and explanatory of the work performed. They may not include all of the duties required of a position and shall not be designed to serve as detailed work assignments.

## Section 10 - COMPENSATION PLAN

Definition: A compensation plan is an organized salary scale established to maintain salary levels consistent with comparable positions, to provide incentives through proper administration of wages, and to ensure that employees are treated consistently and equitably.

Policy: HAMILTON shall develop and maintain an up-to-date compensation plan.

Procedures: 10.1 The Board of Directors shall commission the Chief Operating Officer to develop a compensation plan.

10.2 The Board of Directors shall adopt a compensation plan prepared by the Chief Operating Officer that complies with the Boards' wishes and intentions.

10.3 The Board shall require an annual review and update of the compensation plan.

10.4 The compensation plan shall prescribe the minimum, maximum and intermediate steps of pay appropriate for each position in the Federation.

10.5 The salary range for a position shall reflect required qualifications, duties, and responsibilities and shall be related to compensation for comparable positions in other places of public and private employment within the local job market.

10.6   If the salary range for a position is changed by the Board of Directors, all employees whose positions are re-evaluated shall receive compensation adjustments, which correspond to the steps in the new salary range, unless the Board of Directors specifies exceptions to the compensation adjustments.

7.7   Employees who are performing satisfactorily and are not receiving the maximum salary for the position shall be eligible for advancement to the next higher step in the salary range on their performance evaluation date (see Section 8 of these policies and procedures).

10.8   No salary advancements shall be granted beyond a salary range maximum.

10.9   All salary step advancements shall require the written approval of the Chief Operating Officer. Prior to granting approval the Chief Operating Officer shall consult with the appropriate supervisor to determine whether the employee is performing satisfactorily.

10.10   An employee who is moved to another position in the same class or to another position in another class with the same salary range shall receive no change in salary.

10.11   When employees are moved from one position to another position with a higher maximum salary, their salaries shall be the minimum salary for the new position, unless that minimum is lower than, or the same as, their salary at the time they are moved. In that event, the employee shall receive the next higher step with the pay range for the new position.

10.12 When an employee is demoted, or moved from one position with a lower maximum salary, the Chief Operating Officer shall establish a rate of compensation within the salary range of the class to which the employee has been demoted.

10.13 New employees shall receive the minimum salary for the position for which they are hired, unless the Chief Operating Officer grants an exception for one of the following reasons:

a.      In cases of unusual difficulty in filling a position, the Chief Operating Officer may approve appointment at a salary above the minimum, and;

b.      In hiring exceptionally qualified personnel, the Chief Operating Officer may approve appointment at a salary above the minimum.

10.14 The Chief Operating Officer or his/her designee, shall compare current HAMILTON classifications and compensation plans with those of other public and private employers within the local job market at least once each fiscal year. Changes in the cost of living shall also be considered in light of the local job market.

10.15 The Chief Operating Officer or his/her designee shall examine the salary range for each position to ascertain whether current minimum and maximum salaries should be maintained, increased or decreased during the succeeding fiscal year. Upon the basis of this analysis, the Chief Operating Officer shall submit recommendations for revision of the compensation plan to the Board of Directors.

## Section 11 - PAY PERIODS

Definition: Pay periods are intervals of time in which remuneration will be given for work performed in accordance with all applicable labor laws.

Policy: HAMILTON shall pay employees for work performed.

Procedures: 11.1 Employees shall be paid on a bi-weekly basis, 26 times per calendar year.

11.2 Employees shall be paid on an up-to-date basis for the hours worked. Wages will be withheld for two weeks upon initial employment.

11.3 Standard employee contributions such as local, state and federal taxes will be deducted from paychecks. In addition, deductions may be made for medical insurance and retirement accounts for eligible employees (see Section 13 of these policies and procedures).

11.4 In the case of termination, the employee shall be paid for the hours worked and accrued vacation leave to the effective date of termination. Such payment shall be made on the next scheduled pay date following the date of termination.

11.5 Whenever an employee terminates his or her employment with HAMILTON, the final payment shall be placed in the custody of the Chief Operating Officer, his or her designee, to receive the payment and to participate in a brief exit interview, unless such an appointment is physically impossible.

11.6    HAMILTON shall not garnish an employee's pay unless required by law to do so. HAMILTON will seek monetary reimbursement from an employee if HAMILTON suffers a loss due to clear negligent acts or malfeasance of its employees. This includes the loss of any equipment or other similar property used by HAMILTON.

11.7    In the case of aversive funding or financial hardships, due to either a funding cutback or loss of funding, HAMILTON reserves the right to implement monthly payrolls. This measure should only be executed when no other option is available to management. Employees will be given adequate notice, and those employees choosing not to accept these conditions may at their own discretion resign. By implementing monthly payrolls management will have the opportunity to stabilize the organizations' financial position.

## Section 12 - SALARIES AND WAGES

Definition: Salaries and wages are financial compensations received by employees for work performed.

Policy: HAMILTON shall provide fair remuneration according to established classification and compensation plans.

Procedures: 12.1 Salaries and wages shall be established by the Chief Operating Officer, approved by the Board of Directors, and specified on all job descriptions.

12.2 Salaries and wages shall be based upon the classification of exempt and non-exempt employees (see Section 9 of these policies and procedures).

12.3 For non-exempt employees, overtime shall be defined as any time in excess of 40.0 hours in a calendar week. Overtime must be approved by the employee's supervisor prior to the employee performing same.

12.4 Non-exempt employees shall be eligible for compensation time or overtime remuneration at the rate of one-and-one half hours of pay for each hour worked.

12.5 Non-exempt employees shall select either compensation time or time-and-one-half remuneration for hours in excess of 40.0 hours before said hours are worked.

12.6  Increases in salary or wage compensation may be granted in four ways:

a.  Step Raises: Employees may be given a one-step increase after six months of service and every year after six months of service and every year thereafter. Step increases can only occur when the employee's performance is evaluated as satisfactory or above and the employee has not reached the maximum step in his or her salary grade.

b.  Merit Increases: At the discretion of the Chief Operating Officer, and with the advice and counsel of the employee's supervisor, an employee may be given additional step increases for meritorious or outstanding performance. Meritorious increases shall be awarded at the conclusion of regularly scheduled or commendation performance evaluations (see Section 8 of these policies and procedures).

c.  Promotion: Promotion of an employee to a position in a higher paying job classification shall include an increase in pay.

d.  Cost of Living Adjustment: With the approval of the Board of Directors, the Chief Operating Officer may authorize an across the board increment by adjusting all steps in the current compensation plan. Adjustments shall be made for all employees at the same rate (or percentage) and at the same time.

## Section 13 - FRINGE BENEFITS

Definition: Fringe Benefits are compensations, other than salary, which are given to employees.

Policy: HAMILTON shall provide fringe benefits to eligible employees.

Procedures: 13.1 With the exception of contract employees, all HAMILTON employees shall participate in the following:

a.  State Workmen's Compensation Funds; and;

b.  State Unemployment Insurance Program.

13.2 Permanent full-time employees may be entitled to fringe benefits at a cost not to exceed nineteen percent (19%) of their total annual salary. Said benefits shall include those specified in 13.1 above and life insurance, health insurance, retirement plan and disability benefits.

13.3 Hourly and graduate student employees shall not be eligible for the benefits outlined in (13.2).

13.4 Contract employees shall not be eligible for the benefits outlined in 13.1 or 13.2 above.

13.5 HAMILTON shall pay the full premium cost for group life insurance for permanent full-time employees. Coverage shall be provided for one and one half (1-1/2) times an employee's annual salary up to $100,000.

13.7  HAMILTON may participate in a defined contribution profit sharing plan on behalf of permanent full-time employees. HAMILTON may contribute one percent (1%) of the annual salary of each participating employee to the plan. In addition, participating employees may contribute up to ten percent (5%) of their annual earnings.

13.8  A permanent full-time employee who participates in the defined contribution pension plan outlined in 13.7 above and who becomes disabled shall be eligible to receive all the benefits consistent with the rules of the insurance carrier in his or her pension account.

13.9  A permanent full-time employee who participates in the defined contribution pension plan outlined in 13.7 above and who terminates employment with HAMILTON or withdraws from the plan prior to retirement, shall be entitled to the contribution to the plan. An employee who wishes to terminate participation should contact the Chief Operating Officer for complete information.

13.10  Regular full-time employees may have the discretion to choose a package of benefits and to make changes in such benefits, provided that the total aggregate cost does not exceed 19% specified in 13.2 above. An employee who wishes to change benefit participation should contact the Chief Operating Officer.

13.11   HAMILTON may with the approval of the Board of Directors, change or amend life and medical insurance, pension and (disability plans). However, in doing so, HAMILTON shall strive to improve coverage and shall not deprive any employee of benefits accrued through previous plan participation. The Chief Operating Officer shall notify all employees of any changes in fringe benefits.

13.12   Information concerning all employee benefits, and instructions for filing claims with carriers, shall be available from the Chief Operating Officer or his/her designee.

## Section 14 - VACATION LEAVE

Definition: Vacation leave is a benefit extended to employees for rest and relaxation.

Policy: HAMILTON shall provide vacation leave to eligible employees.

Procedures: 14.1 Regular full-time employees in positions classified as exempt shall accumulate vacation leave on the following basis:

| Years of Service | Vacation Leave |
|---|---|
| 1 - 3 years | 2 weeks |
| 4 - 10 years | 4 weeks |
| 11 - 20 years | 5 weeks |

14.2 Permanent full-time employees in positions classified as non-exempt accumulate vacation on the following basis:

| Years of Service | Vacation Leave |
|---|---|
| 1 - 5 years | 2 weeks |
| 6 - 10 years | 3 weeks |
| 11 - 20 years | 4 weeks |

14.3 Hourly, graduate student and contract employees shall not be eligible for vacation leave.

14.4   Eligible employees shall accumulate vacation leave from the date of hire, but vacation leave may not be utilized during the first six months of probationary employee status.

14.5   At the conclusion of a year of service, permanent full-time employees in exempt and non-exempt positions, with the exception of the Executive Director and Chief Operating Officer, may be permitted to carry up to ten (10) days of unused vacation time to the next succeeding year. Permission to carry over unused vacation time must be obtained in writing from the Chief Operating Officer.

14.6   For vacations of three (3) or more days, the employee shall request vacation time in writing from the Chief Operating Officer at least three (3) weeks in advance of the initial day of vacation. Failure to request vacation in advance may result in denial of the request.

14.7   The Chief Operating Officer shall schedule all vacations with due respect for the requirements of HAMILTON and the needs of employees.

14.8   Vacation time granted shall not exceed time accrued.

14.9   Vacation leave may be charged on the basis of one hour of vacation leave for each hour absent.

14.10   Vacation time may be taken in increments of no less than four (4) hours.

14.11 The pay rate applied for vacation leave shall be equivalent to the employee's normal rate of pay, as if he or she had actually worked.

14.12 If a legal holiday designated in Section 16 of these policies and procedures falls within an employee's vacation leave, it shall not be charged to vacation leave.

14.13 When an employee terminates with HAMILTON, he or she shall be reimbursed for any accrued but unused vacation leave.

## Section 15 - SICK LEAVE

Definition: Sick leave is time granted away from work for employees who are ill.

Policy: HAMILTON shall grant time off for sick leave.

Procedures: 15.1 Full-time regular employees shall earn sick leave with full pay at the rate of 1.25 days for each month worked (15 days for each twelve-months of service).

15.2 Hourly, graduate students and contract employees shall not be eligible for sick leave with pay, unless stipulated in writing by the Chief Operating Officer.

15.3 Sick leave shall accrue from the date of employment for permanent full-time employees and may not be used during the probationary period.

15.4 Employees shall be eligible for sick leave for the following reasons:

    a. non-occupational personal illness;

    b. quarantine of an employee by a physician for an illness unrelated to occupation;

    c. dental, optical or other physical or medical examinations or treatments; and,

d. illness in the immediate family, which requires that the employee remain at home.

15.5 Sick leave shall be charged on the basis of one hour of sick leave for each hour absent.

15.6 Sick leave may not be taken in increments of less than one (1) hour.

15.7 An employee who is unable to report to work due to a reason outlined in 15.4 above shall notify the immediate supervisor or the Chief Operating Officer no later than one (4) hours from the time he or she is expected to report for work. When the report of illness is called in, it is the responsibility of security or the immediate supervisor to log in this information and upon the employees return to work he or she must verify that the proper documentation of their call was made accordingly. Sick leave with pay shall not be allowed unless such a report is made and this procedure is followed.

15.8 For an illness that lasts more than three (3) days, an employee may be required to submit verification of illness from a licensed physician to the Chief Operating Officer or his/her designee.

15.9 If an employee has used all sick leave prior to the end of the calendar year, he or she may ask the Chief Operating Officer for permission to use vacation or personal time for sick leave. Permission shall be granted at the discretion of the Chief Operating Officer.

15.10   At the conclusion of a year of service, an employee may not carry-over unused sick leave to the succeeding year unless authorized by the Chief Operating Officer.

15.11   Abuse of sick leave privileges shall be cause for disciplinary action (see Section 21 of the policies and procedures).

15.12   Upon termination with HAMILTON, an employee shall not be compensated for unused sick leave.

15.13   While an employee is out on sick leave, vacation time and sick leave time will not be accrued in that there is no compensational work being performed.

15.14   Physicians may not write his/her own note if he/she has been out sick for any period of time.

## Section 16 - PERSONAL LEAVE

Definition: Personal leave is time granted to employees to attend to private matters.

Policy: HAMILTON shall provide personal leave to eligible employees.

Procedures: 16.1 Regular full-time employees in exempt and non-exempt positions shall be provided with three (3) personal days per year.

16.2 Personal leave shall be accrued from the date of hire and may not be used during the probationary employment period and this time is prorated.

16.3 Hourly, graduate and student and contract employees shall not be eligible for personal leave, unless specified in writing by the Chief Operating Officer.

16.4 Personal leave shall be taken in increments of less than one (1) day.

16.5 Personal leave shall be charged on the basis of one day of personal leave for each day absent.

16.6 The pay rate applied to personal leave shall be equivalent to the employee's normal rate of pay, as if he or she had actually worked.

16.7   If it is possible, an employee shall request advanced written permission to utilize leave from the Chief Operating Officer. If it is not possible to provide advance notice, the employee shall contact his or her immediate supervisor or the Chief Operating Officer within one (1) hour of the time he or she is expected to report for work.

16.8   At the conclusion of a year of service, an employee may not carry-over unused personal leave to the succeeding year unless authorized by the Chief Operating Officer.

16.9   When an employee terminates with HAMILTON he or she shall be compensated for accrued leave but not for unused personal leave.

## Section 17 - HOLIDAYS

Definition: Holidays are special days of compensation.

Policy: HAMILTON shall grant time off to employees to observe designated holidays.

Procedures: 17.1 The following national holidays shall be observed by HAMILTON.

- New Year's Day
- Martin Luther King's Birthday
- President's Day
- Memorial Day
- Independence Day
- Labor Day
- Easter
- Columbus Day
- Veteran's Day
- Thanksgiving Day
- Christmas Day

17.2 If a holiday designated above falls on a Saturday, it shall be observed on the preceding Friday. If a holiday designated above falls on a Sunday, it shall be observed on the following Monday.

17.3 All full-time regular employees shall be compensated for holidays. Hourly, contract and graduate student employees shall not be compensated.

17.4   A non-exempt employee who must work on a holiday shall be compensated in one of two ways: through equal time off or through monetary compensation at one-and-one-half times the employee's rate of pay. The Chief Operating Officer and the employee shall establish the method of compensation before said holiday.

17.5   Holidays that occur during an employee's vacation leave shall not be charged against such leave.

17.6   Eligible employees shall be compensated for holidays from the date-of-hire.

17.7   A new employee who reports to work the day after a paid holiday shall not be compensated for that holiday.

17.8   When an employee terminates on the last working day before a holiday, he or she shall not be paid for that holiday.

17.9   An employee who is on leave of absence without pay shall not be paid for holidays.

17.10   Election days shall not be considered holidays, but employees may be given necessary time to vote in accordance with New Jersey statutes.

17.11   HAMILTON shall issue a schedule of holidays to employees at the beginning of each calendar year.

17.12  Employees who wish to observe religious holidays may request permission in writing from the Chief Operating Officer. Observance of these holidays shall be charged to annual leave.

17.13  If an employee becomes ill during a holiday, the employee will not be credited with sick leave and if an employee calls in ill the day before and/or after a holiday, a doctor's verification must be presented. Failure to do so may result in loss of pay.

## Section 18 - LEAVES OF ABSENCE

Definition: A leave of absence is an approved block of time in which an employee will not be working for HAMILTON.

Policy: HAMILTON may grant leaves of absence for specific reasons.

Procedures: 18.1 <u>Illness or Accident</u>: An employee who, because of illness or accident, is deemed incapable of returning to work by medical professionals may be granted a leave of absence (see Section 13 of these policies and procedures).

Approval of said leave shall be contingent upon 1) notification of the Chief Operating Officer and, 2) receipt of recommendations from a licensed physician. The Chief Operating Officer shall grant final approval of said leave. Employees may be required to undergo a physical examination at the discretion of the Chief Operating Officer when, in his or her opinion, an employee is incapable of adequate job performance.

The Chief Operating Officer may designate the examining physician and HAMILTON shall assume costs. In such cases, the Chief Operating Officer may require an employee to take a sick leave for a period consistent with the examining physician's examination. After twelve weeks leave of absence for a disability or illness, HAMILTON may fill a vacated position on either temporary or permanent basis. If a position is filled on a permanent basis, HAMILTON shall put the disabled or ill employee on a preferential list for hire to the first available permanent position for which the employee is qualified.

18.2    Family Leave: Any regular employee is entitled to family leave of 12 weeks in any 24 month period after advance notice to HAMILTON. In the case of a seriously ill child, parent or spouse, employees may take the leave intermittently so long as 12 weeks taken does not exceed 12 months for each serious health condition. Leave, which is taken as a result of the birth or placement for adoption of a child, may begin at any time within a year of the birth or placement. In addition to the 12 weeks of family leave, maternity leave will be granted for the birth or placement of any adopted baby for an additional 1-1/2 months beginning any time up to three months prior to the anticipated birth of a baby (in the case of a birth) or sooner if the necessity of which is verified by a physician. If an employee requests a return to work after the allowed for five- and one-half month period of family and maternity leave specified above, HAMILTON shall make every effort to place the employee in the same, or in a comparable position as that from which leave was granted. Reinstatement at that point, however, will be provided at the discretion of the Chief Operating Officer, and shall be made in light of budget guidelines and the needs of HAMILTON.

18.3    Jury Duty and Witness Participation: The Chief Operating Officer shall grant time off to employees for the performance of jury duty. In such cases, HAMILTON shall reimburse the employee for the difference between his or her normal rate of pay and the per diem jury rate. The employee shall provide the Chief Operating Officer with written documentation of the rate of pay for jury duty. An employee who is required to serve as a witness in a municipal, county, state or federal court shall provide written documentation of court participation to the Chief Operating Officer of HAMILTON. HAMILTON will reimburse said employee at his or her normal rate of pay. When an employee must participate as a juror or witness in a long-term judicial proceeding, HAMILTON may request that said employee make arrangements to be absent from work only when absolutely necessary.

18.4   <u>Military Reserve and Active Duty:</u> Leaves of absence shall be granted so that employees may complete annual field training and related obligations with the National Guard and other branches of the Armed Forces Reserves. Application for military reserve leave of absence must be made as soon as possible after an employee receives military orders. HAMILTON shall reimburse an employee for the difference between his or her normal rate of pay and that offered by the reserve forces.

Employees who enter active military service shall notify the Chief Operating Officer in writing as soon as possible after the receipt of orders. The Chief Operating Officer in compliance with all applicable provisions and legislation shall reinstate said employees to the same or similar positions.

18.5    Funeral Leave:

In the event of a death in the employee's immediate family, he or she may be granted a leave of absence. For the purpose of this provision, immediate family shall be defined as father, mother, sister, brother, spouse, children, parent-in-law, grandparents and grand children. Funeral leaves shall not exceed three (3) consecutive working days. This provision does not apply if the death occurs during an employee's paid vacation or while the employee is on leave of absence for another reason.

Should funeral leave exceed the three day allocation specified above, the Chief Operating Officer may authorize that additional leave be taken from accumulated sick, personal or vacation leave or as a leave of absence without pay. Funeral leave requested for persons other than immediate family shall be granted at the discretion of the Chief Operating Officer.

18.6    General Provisions:

    a.  For the purpose of granting leaves of absence, a working day shall be equal to eight (8.0) hours.

    b.  The leaves of absence outlined in 18.1 through 18.5 above shall be available only to permanent full-time employees, unless otherwise specified in writing.

    c.  With the exception of emergency illness/accident leaves, all requests for leaves of absence must be submitted in advance to the Chief Operating Officer or his/her designee.

## Section 19 - CAREER DEVELOPMENT

Definition: Career development activities are training and educational events, which promote the personal and professional growth of employees and which, therefore, enhance the quality of HAMILTON service.

Policy: HAMILTON shall encourage personnel to participate in career development activities.

Procedures: 19.1 Individuals must be employed by HAMILTON for one full calendar year to qualify for participation in career development activities. Employees may be allowed up to ten (10) working days for career development activities during each subsequent year of employment.

19.2 Participation in career development activities must be approved by the Chief Operating Officer. Approval shall be made on the basis of employee responsibilities, HAMILTON needs, operational demands, and the availability of funds.

19.3 HAMILTON may mandate participation in specific career development activities for an employee. The need for said activities must be reflected in an employee's performance evaluation.

19.4 Employees may request permission to participate in training and education programs directly related to job responsibilities. Requests must be submitted in writing to the Chief Operating Officer as soon as possible and no later than ten (10) working days prior to the training or educational program.

19.5　HAMILTON may reimburse tuition for courses directly related to an employee's job responsibilities. Reimbursement shall be made provided that a) funds for such expenditures are available in the current budget; b) the employee has made application to the Chief Operating Officer for the approval of tuition reimbursement prior to registration for such courses; and, c) the employee submits evidence of satisfactory completion of the course to the Chief Operating Officer no later than 30 days after its conclusion. This policy is subject to budget restrictions. HAMILTON reserves the right to suspend tuition reimbursement at any time prior to an employee actually taking a class. However, HAMILTON will honor all written commitments.

19.6　Reimbursement for courses shall be based upon the following scale:

| Grade Received in the Course | Percent of Reimbursement |
| --- | --- |
| A | 100% |
| B | 80% |
| C | 50% |
| D | 0% |
| F | 0% |

For courses or training in which no grade is given, reimbursement shall be made at the discretion of the Chief Operating Officer based upon evidence of satisfactory completion of the course or training (i.e., certificates, diploma).

19.7  If an employee withdraws from a course, HAMILTON shall not reimburse the employee for said course.

19.8  Employees who receive financial aid from sources outside HAMILTON shall submit written documentation of said aid to the Chief Operating Officer. Reimbursement from all sources shall not exceed 100% of the actual cost.

19.9  The cost of textbooks and technical publications required for courses shall be the responsibility of the employee, unless HAMILTON purchases the publications as resource materials.

19.10  At a future date, HAMILTON may have the resources to grant educational leaves of absence to employees. If said resources do become available, HAMILTON shall incorporate them into Section 18 of these policies and procedures.

## Section 20 - REIMBURSEMENT FOR TRAVEL

Definition:   This Section concerns travel, which is required of an employee in the line of duty.

Policy: HAMILTON shall reimburse employees for travel that is required for successful completion of job responsibilities:

Procedures:   20.1   When an employee must take a trip for which expenses will be in excess of $40.00, the employee shall submit a written travel plan to the Chief Operating Officer no less than two weeks in advance of the departure date, if possible. The employee shall also submit a Weekly Expense Report form to the Chief Operating Officer within three (3) working days of completion of said travel.

20.2   When an employee must make a trip for which total expenses will exceed $250.00, the employee may request an advance from the Chief Operating Officer. The request should be submitted in writing as early as possible. The employee shall also submit a Weekly Expense Report to the Chief Operating Officer within three (3) working days of completion of said travel. The Report shall include a full account of the use of the advance and all other reimbursable expenses.

20.3   When an employee must make a trip for which expenses will be less than $250.00, the employee shall submit a Weekly Expense

Report form to the Chief Operating Officer within three (3) working days of the completion of said travel.

20.4   Weekly Expense Reports shall include receipts for transportation, lodging, meals and other expenditures that can be documented.

20.5   Employees shall be reimbursed for mileage at the rate of $.35 per mile.

20.6   Employees shall take advantage of pre-registration and early travel and hotel confirmation savings whenever possible. In addition, employees shall be expected to utilize economy class travel arrangements. If an employee wishes to utilize first-class travel arrangements, he or she shall be responsible for the monetary difference between economy and first-class fares.

20.7   Employees are expected to keep travel expenses within reason, and allowances for lodging, meals and other items shall be made at the discretion of the Chief Operating Officer. See financial policy and procedures Travel Section.

## Section 21 - EMPLOYEE GRIEVANCES

Definition: A grievance is any dispute or complaint regarding the meaning, interpretation, application or alleged violation of the terms and provisions of existing policies and procedures.

Policy: HAMILTON shall provide a grievance policy to review, mediate and resolve complaints concerning discrimination or employment conditions.

Procedures: 21.1 The following procedures shall apply to each phase of the grievance process.

- a. In the event that a grievance is not responded to within the time limits established in this section, either party (employee or supervisor) may take the grievance to the next level of appeal. Exceptions to time limits may be made only by mutual agreement and agreements to extend time limits shall be documented in writing and signed by all parties involved.
- b. All discussions concerning complaints shall be held in the strictest of confidence.
- c. Supervisors shall not make adverse comments or threats to an employee who has filed a complaint.
- d. No individual shall be intimidated, threatened, coerced or discriminated against for filing a complaint, for furnishing information, or for participating in any manner

in an investigation, compliance review, hearing or any other activity related to the administration of the policies and procedures governing the employment or advancement of employees.

e. Any supervisor who receives a complaint filed by an employee through a government agency or through outside legal counsel shall immediately inform the Chief Operating Officer. The Chief Operating Officer shall immediately inform HAMILTON legal counsel for review of said complaint.

f. Once an employee has filed a formal complaint with an outside agency or legal counsel, no supervisor shall discuss the complaint with the employee under any circumstances. No information concerning said employee is to be disseminated in any form.

21.2   Supervisors and employees are expected to resolve problems as they arise on an informal basis whenever possible.

21.3   If employees are reluctant to discuss a matter with their supervisor, upon a written request they may speak with the Chief Operating Officer. The Chief Operating Officer shall answer an employee's questions about HAMILTON policy only.

21.4   <u>Informal grievance:</u>   An employee who has a complaint which has not been resolved through 21.3 above, must discuss the matter with his or her supervisor either within five (5) regularly scheduled working days after the employee became aware of the event. The supervisor shall provide the employee with an oral response within five (5) regularly scheduled working days after the complaint is lodged. If the employee and supervisor are unable to reach an acceptable agreement the employee may file a formal grievance to the Chief Operating Officer.

21.5    In the event that a grievance cannot be resolved through informal grievance process defined in 21.4 above, the employee may file a formal grievance with the Chief Operating Officer. The formal grievance must be submitted within five (5) regularly scheduled working days of the completion of the informal grievance procedure.

21.6    <u>Formal Grievance:</u> Formal grievances shall be submitted in writing and shall include a description of:

a. What occurred;

b. When it occurred;

c. Where it occurred;

d. Who was affected;

e. Which sections of HAMILTON policies and procedures allegedly have been violated and;

f. What adjustment or actions are requested.

21.7 The Chief Operating Officer shall within ten (10) regularly scheduled working days, mediate the grievance with the employee, immediate supervisor and/or any other individuals involved, and shall attempt to resolve the grievance to mutual satisfaction. Facts leading up to the grievance and recommendations for corrective actions shall be recorded and signed by all parties involved.

21.8 Grievances regarding termination of employment may be further appealed to the Board of Directors if the employee or supervisor is not satisfied with the decision of the Chief Operating Officer in response to a formal grievance. Either party may appeal a decision regarding termination in writing within five (5) regular scheduled working days of the determination of the Chief Operating Officer. The written appeal should be submitted to the President of the Board of Directors.

    a. The President of the Board of Directors shall, within ten (10) regularly scheduled working days, mediate the grievance with the employee, immediate supervisor and other persons involved and shall attempt to resolve the grievance to mutual satisfaction. Facts leading up to the grievance and the recommendation of the Chairperson of the Board of Directors recorded and signed by all parties involved.

    b. If the employee or supervisor is not satisfied with the report of the Chairman of the Board of Directors either party may appeal in writing to the full Board of Directors within five (5) regularly scheduled working days of the Chairman's report.

c. The Board of Directors shall, within ten (10) regularly scheduled working days, mediate the grievance with the employee, immediate supervisor, and other individuals involved and shall attempt to resolve the grievance to mutual satisfaction. Facts leading up to the grievance and the recommendations of the Board of Directors shall be recorded and signed by all parties involved. The decision of the Board of Directors shall be final. The employee will have a right to have counsel participate at this stage of the procedure.

21.9 If the employee is not satisfied with the decision of the Board of Directors, he/she may seek legal redress but only after all the above administrative procedures are exhausted.

21.10 If the Executive Director or Chief Operating Officer has a grievance, he or she may appeal in writing to the President of the Board of Directors. The Chief Operating Officer must appeal in writing within ten (10) regularly scheduled working days of the actual occurrence, of his or her knowledge of the occurrence, of the incident on which the grievance is based.

21.11 The Chairman of the Board of Directors, shall within ten (10) regularly scheduled working days, mediate the grievance with the Executive Director or Chief Operating Officer and other persons involved and shall attempt to resolve the grievance to mutual satisfactions. Facts leading up to the grievance and the recommendations of the Chairperson of the Board of Directors shall be recorded and signed by all parties involved.

21.12  If the Executive Director or Chief Operating Officer is not satisfied with the report of the Chairman of the Board of Directors, he or she may appeal in writing to the full Board of Directors within ten (10) scheduled working days of the Chairman's report.

21.13  The Board of Directors shall, within ten (10) regularly scheduled working days, mediate the grievance with the Executive Director or Chief Operating Officer and other persons involved and shall attempt to resolve the grievance to mutual satisfaction. Facts leading up to the grievance and the recommendations of the Board of Directors shall be recorded and signed by all parties involved. The decision of the Board of Directors shall be final.

21.14  If the Executive Director or Chief Operating Officer is not satisfied with the decision of the Board of Directors, he or she may seek legal redress.

## Section 22 - DISCIPLINARY ACTIONS

Definition: Disciplinary actions are procedures, which will be implemented to correct and/or control violations of HAMILTON policies and procedures.

Policy: HAMILTON will take disciplinary action when an employee's conduct and/or performance falls below established standards.

Procedures: 22.1 In order for HAMILTON to meet its' needs and goals it is necessary to establish and maintain standards of conduct for employees. Certain conduct by employees is counterproductive of the agency's goals, interferes with a harmonious work environment and cannot be tolerated. The following list is intended to illustrate the type of conduct that is prohibited and which will be addressed with disciplinary measures.

a. Neglect of duty, or refusal to comply with management's lawful instructions, unless such instructions are injurious to the employee, to the general public health or safety, or are contrary to the employee's professional code of ethics.

b. Insubordination or deliberate refusal to comply with a supervisor's specific directions, or encouraging others to refuse to comply, deliberate attempts to undermine a supervisor's authority, or derisive or disruptive behavior leading to dissension among staff or otherwise negatively affecting staff performance.

c. Immoral or indecent conduct involving public censure or conviction of a felony, or a misdemeanor involving moral turpitude, while an employee of HAMILTON.

d. Violations of confidential information concerning HAMILTON business members or personnel, its business affairs, personnel records and patient records.

e. Indulging in offensive or abusive conduct or using offensive and/or abusive language towards the public or toward HAMILTON members or staff.

f. Intentional falsification of personnel records or HAMILTON reports or attempts to conceal falsification by other employees, including time cards and time sheets and employment applications.

g. Incompetence and inefficiency in the performance of job duties. Declining performance or a noticeable decrease in work output to a level below requirements set for job performance and/or failure to cooperate with other employees. Cooperation is essential to effective program operations.

h. Unprofessional behavior or display of personal attitudes, which indicate a lack of respect for the importance of a productive working environment.

I. Carelessness or neglect with the money or properties of HAMILTON, theft or intentional destruction of HAMILTON property or another employee's property. This includes, but is not limited to supplies and equipment and the personal belongings of HAMILTON members, staff and visitors.

j.      Reporting to work under the influence of alcohol, drugs or other mood-altering substances, or the use of such substances while on duty.

k.      Deliberate or careless conduct endangering the safety of self or others, including violence or threats of violence, concealing an infectious disease and failure to promptly report on-the-job accidents to the Chief Operating Officer and/or authorities.

l.      Deliberate, unauthorized release of material to the mass media which results in harm to HAMILTON, to its members, or to its employees.

m.      Inducing, or attempting to induce, an employee in the service of HAMILTON to commit an unlawful act or to act in violation of any law, regulation, order or professional ethic.

n.      Attempting or threatening to use personal or political influence in an effort to secure special consideration as a HAMILTON employee.

o.      Accepting any fee, gift or other valuable object for personal use when the fee, gift or object is given in the hope of receiving a favor or preferential treatment from HAMILTON.

p.      Absence from work without permission of the immediate supervisor.

q. Excessive absenteeism and/or tardiness.

r. Violation of any of the policies and procedures of HAMILTON.

22.2 HAMILTON may discipline employees who engage in any of the aforesaid types of conduct or other improper behavior counterproductive to the efficient operation of HAMILTON in meeting its' goals. Disciplinary action may range from oral reprimand, written reprimands, suspension with or without pay, demotion to termination depending upon the gravity and frequency of the offense. The type of disciplinary action taken to respond to such conduct is with the sole discretion of HAMILTON.

22.3 A regular full-time or hourly employee who is subject to disciplinary action may invoke the grievance procedures outlined in Section 20 of these policies and procedures.

22.4 All written notices concerning disciplinary actions shall be provided in duplicate by the Chief Operating Officer. The first copy shall be given to the employee and the second shall be signed by the employee as evidence of delivery. The second copy shall be placed in the employee's personnel file.

22.5 If an employee is not cited for additional disciplinary actions and is rated satisfactory or above on performance evaluations, the written record of a disciplinary action shall be removed from his or her personnel file after two years.

## 22.6 Dress Code:

The employees of HAMILTON shall dress in a manner befitting their particular assignment and at all times reflecting the professionalism that HAMILTON represents.

a.  MAINTENANCE UNIFORM: (Men and Women) Provided by HAMILTON will be Navy blue pants and light blue shirts to be worn inside the pants and belted. Short sleeve shirts may be worn during the summer months and long sleeves during the winter. Proper working shoes are to be worn. Slippers and sandals are unacceptable.

b.  Working gloves are provided by HAMILTON and if lost or stolen must be replaced at employee's expense.

c.  Females are expected to wear business attire, with skirt length no shorter than two (2) inches above the knees. Stretch pants, spandex skirts very low cut blouses or dresses, fish net and herring bone stockings cut at the ankles, slippers and sandals are unacceptable. Shorts, sneakers and socks are unacceptable while on duty. However, on a designated dress down day, blue jeans may be worn.

d.  Males and females who wear uniforms must be in full uniform while on duty. Lab coats (provided by HAMILTON) must be worn by all employees who attend to patients in the clinical area. HAMILTON will provide initial lab coat, should it be lost or stolen, employee must replace it at his or her own expense.

## Section 23 - SUSPENSION

Definition: Suspension is an action taken to hold an employee's position in an undecided state for a specific period of time.

Policy: HAMILTON may suspend employees with or without pay.

Procedures: 23.1 The Chief Operating Officer and his/her designee have the authority to suspend an employee without pay or benefits when job performance or conduct justifies disciplinary action short of dismissal (see Section 22 of these policies and procedures).

23.2 Regular full-time and hourly employees shall be entitled to a hearing as outlined in Section 21 of these policies and procedures if suspended.

23.4 Suspension shall not last more than thirty (30) calendar days unless the Chief Operating Officer finds good cause to extend the period. The Chief Operating Officer shall use his sole discretion in making this determination.

23.5 The Chief Operating Officer or his/her designee shall give the employee verbal notice. Written notice shall be provided within 24 hours. The notice shall state the reasons for the suspension and its duration.

23.6 Written notice of suspension shall be placed in the employee's personnel file.

## Section 24 - DEMOTION

Definition: Demotion is the movement of an employee to a lower position in the HAMILTON classification plan.

Policy: Employees may be demoted for disciplinary and non-disciplinary reasons.

Procedures: 24.1 The Chief Operating Officer may reassign an employee to a class with a lower maximum salary for the following reasons:

    a. inability to carry out the necessary duties required for that particular position; and

    b. disciplinary reasons, as titled in Section 22 of these policies and procedures; and

    c. failure to comply with performance review stipulations and directives.

24.2 Any employee may be subject to non-disciplinary demotion in the situations listed below:

    a. when an employee's position is reclassified or reassigned to a lower pay grade;

    b. when an employee requests a demotion with the Chief Operating Officer's approval;

c. when an employee's position is abolished because workload or funds have decreased;

d. when an employee is displaced by the return to work of an employee from a leave of absence. For example, a former regular employee returning from military service would be entitled to reinstatement under the provisions in Section 17 of these policies and procedures.

24.3 Non-disciplinary demotions shall be made with the consent of the employee, provided that the employee possesses the qualifications required for the positions for which he or she is demoted.

24.4 The Chief Operating Officer also has the right to revert an exempt employee to a consultant position and to have the employee execute an appropriate consulting agreement. The Chief Operating Officer will give the reasons for a consulting agreement in writing at least five (5) business days before the effective date.

24.5 An employee shall be notified in writing by the Chief Operating Officer at least two (2) weeks before a non-disciplinary demotion becomes effective.

24.6 The Chief Operating Officer shall give the employee written notice of a disciplinary demotion no later than one (1) day before it takes effect. The notice shall include the reasons for the demotion.

24.7 Written notice of demotion shall be placed in the employee's personnel file.

24.8    Regular full-time and hourly employees have the right to appeal disciplinary demotions (see Section 21 of these policies and procedures).

## Section 25 - TERMINATION

Definition: Termination is an action taken by either HAMILTON or the employee in order to conclude employment.

Policy: This Section is based upon the following policies:

a. Employees may be terminated either voluntarily or involuntarily. The employment relationship with HAMILTON is <u>at-will</u>. HAMILTON can <u>terminate</u> any employee *with or without cause*. This is a policy that applies to all employees. This policy is not subject to interpretation or speculation. The employer and employee relationship is strictly <u>at-will</u>.

b. All HAMILTON positions are maintained based upon the availability of funds. While, with the exceptions of the Executive Director and Chief Operating Officer, contractual commitments are <u>not</u> made with employees. HAMILTON strives to provide stable and reasonably secure positions to its employees.

Procedures: 25.1 An employee separating from HAMILTON of his or her volition shall provide the Chief Operating Officer and his or her supervisor with a minimum of two weeks written notice.

a. A resignation may be rescinded only with the permission of the Chief Operating Officer and after consultation with the employee's immediate supervisor.

b. A resigning employee may not set his or her termination date on a holiday.

c. A resigning employee shall work through the effective date of his or her termination.

d. Employee must give a two-week notice of resignation or forfeit sick or annual time credit for reimbursement.

25.2   Involuntary Termination: Involuntary termination of personnel, except for the Executive Director and Chief Operating Officer, shall be the responsibility of the Chief Operating Officer. An employee may be dismissed whenever, in the judgment of the Chief Operating Officer, and with or without the advice and counsel of the immediate supervisor, the employee's work or conduct so warrants (see Section 21 of these policies and procedures). Also prior to the involuntary termination of an employee, and employee's tenure with HAMILTON and work history, i.e. evaluations must be considered. Involuntary termination of the Executive Director and Chief Operating Officer shall be the responsibility of the Board of Directors. Termination without notice and without pay in lieu of notice can occur under the following circumstances:

1. Insubordination or noncompliance;

2. Inability to carry out duties as defined in the employee's job description;

3. Inability and/or unwillingness to carry out job functions with a positive attitude toward the agency;

4. Acts committed to undermine and malign the agency;

5. Chronic lateness or absenteeism;

6. Dishonesty, theft;

7. Commission by the employee of any act during the course of employment that constitutes a crime or the act of a disorderly person within the meaning of Title 2-A of the NJSA;

8. Conviction of a crime, civil or criminal;

9. Conviction under the disorderly persons law of an offense directed against a second party;

10. Client abuse or gross negligence or dereliction of duty;

11. Willfully destroying or damaging any property of the facility, clients or other staff members;

12. Disorderly, indecent or immoral conduct;

13. Reporting for or attempting to work while under the influence of, or addicted to a alcohol, drugs, or narcotics or in a physical condition making it unsafe to continue working or possession of drugs or alcohol while on the job;

14. Altering, falsifying or making willful misstatements of fact on an employment application or any other official work record;

15. Violations of confidential information concerning HAMILTON, its personnel, business affairs, or personnel records as defined in Section 1a;

16. Carelessness with the property of HAMILTON;

17. Deliberate unauthorized release of information to the mass media, which results in harm to HAMILTON or to its employees;

18. Attempting or threatening to use personal or political influence in an effort to secure special consideration as a HAMILTON employee;

19. Accepting any fee, gift or other valuable object for personal use when the fee, gift or object is given in the hope of receiving a favor or preferential treatment from HAMILTON;

20. Absence from work without permission of the administrative director or immediate supervisor;

21. Violation of any of HAMILTON's policies and procedures.

25.3    Staff Reduction Due to Budget Cutbacks:

Staff members may be separated from HAMILTON due to the lack of funds or curtailment of a program. If a staff reduction is necessary, the Chief Operating Officer shall provide employees with written notice no less than five (5) working days prior to the effective date of separation. Whenever a reduction is necessary, retention of staff members may be based upon job responsibilities and needs of HAMILTON.

25.4    Procedures Applicable to all Terminations:

a. HAMILTON shall reimburse terminating employees for any accrued but unused vacation time.

b. The Chief Operating Officer shall make every effort to complete a financial settlement between the employee and HAMILTON on the pay date immediately following the effective date of termination. Settlement shall be completed within two regularly scheduled pay dates following the date of termination.

c. Written documentation of all termination actions shall be placed in the employee's personnel file.

d. HAMILTON shall notify the New Jersey unemployment office of all termination actions, upon written request.

## Section 26 - NEPOTISM

Definition: Nepotism consists of placing family members into positions in which one relative exercises decision-making or supervisory authority over another.

Policy: No individual at HAMILTON shall hold a position in which a member of his or her immediate family exercises decision-making or supervisory authority. For the purposes of this policy, a member of an immediate family shall include the following persons:

- husband           grandparents
- wife              grandchildren
- father            father-in-law
- mother            mother-in-law
- brother           brother-in-law
- sister            sister-in-law
- son               son-in-law
- daughter          daughter-in-law
- step-child

Procedures: 26.1 A member of the immediate family of an individual on the Board of Directors may not be employed by HAMILTON.

26.2 A member of the immediate family of an employee may be hired as long as one family member does not exercise decision-making or supervisory authority over another family member.

26.4　A member of the immediate family of an employee may be hired in a position in which both family members report to the same supervisor within a department or an area.

26.5　If a family member is hired by deception, both employees may be subject to termination or other disciplinary action.

## Section 27 - CONFLICT OF INTEREST

Definition: Conflicts of interest may occur when a member of the Board of Directors, Executive Director, or the Chief Operating Officer, or any member of the immediate family of such person obtains a benefit through the purchase of rental goods, space or services by HAMILTON.

Policy: Members of the Board of Directors, Executive Director and the Chief Operating Officer are obligated to advise the Board if a proposed procurement of goods, space or services by HAMILTON creates a potential conflict of interest for him or her; and, said Board members, Executive Director or Chief Operating Officer may not thereafter deliberate and/or vote on any such proposal.

a. the Executive Director and Chief Operating Officer of HAMILTON;

b. any other HAMILTON employee whose responsibilities include the procurement of goods, space or services; and,

c. any individual who is a member of the immediate family of a Board member, Executive Director or a HAMILTON employee (see Section 26 of these policies and procedures for the definition of immediate family members).

27.2 The term "substantial interest" shall be defined as:

a. Any direct or indirect financial interest in the specific sale or rental transaction, including a commission or fee, a share of the proceeds, the prospect of promotion, or any other form of financial interest.

b. Interests in the business, which is supplying the goods, space or services to HAMILTON, including:

- ownership;
- partnership interest or other monetary interest;
- ownership of stock in the business;
- employment with the business; or
- membership on the Board of Directors or other governing body of said business;
- consultation fee.

27.3 This policy addresses personnel and institutional services, including banking, financial, medical, legal, management and consultant services, as well as other types of skilled and unskilled labor.

27.4 The procedures outlined above shall not apply to:

a. Purchases or rentals of goods, space or services from the same supplier at a total cost of less than $10,000 within any twelve month period;

b. Purchases or rental of goods or services if there is no other supplier within a fifty-mile radius of HAMILTON.

c. Purchase of rental of goods, space or services from the lowest bidder, in accordance with the rules for advertised competitive bidding.

d. Purchases or rentals of goods at the lowest price offered by all local suppliers; or,

e. Purchases of services or rentals of goods or space from public or private non-profit organizations at cost, or at standard rates.

## Section 28 - SAFETY AND ACCIDENT PREVENTION

Definition: Safety and accident prevention measures are precautions taken by HAMILTON and its employees to remain free from danger, risk and injury.

Policy: HAMILTON shall maintain a safe working environment for its' employees.

Procedures: 28.1 If employees observe unsafe conditions, equipment or practices, they are expected to report them to the Clinic Director immediately.

28.2 All staff shall be instructed to obtain first aid immediately in the event of an accident. After first aid has been obtained, employees shall contact his or her supervisor as soon as possible.

28.3 If the Clinic Director is not on the premises, the employee shall notify the Operations Manager of the accident as soon as possible.

28.4 If the accident occurs when the Clinic Director is not on the premises, staff shall notify him or her as soon as possible and no later than the next working day. If the Operations Manager cannot be reached, the staff shall notify the Chief Operating Officer no later than one working day after the accident.

28.5 The Operations Manager shall prepare an accident report no later than five (5) working days after an accident. The Chief Operating Officer shall present the report to the Board of Directors within one (1) month of completion of the report. The report shall include recommendations concerning actions, which may enhance employee safety.

28.6　Upon approval by the Board of Directors, the Chief Operating Officer shall implement actions that will prevent accidents and enhance employee safety.

## Section 29 - EMPLOYEE ASSISTANCE

Definition: Employee assistance is provided to individuals who are experiencing personal and/or emotional problems.

Policy: HAMILTON shall provide assistance to troubled employees.

Procedures: 29.1 An employee experiencing personal and/or emotional difficulties may contact the Clinic Director or immediate supervisor for assistance, information and referral.

29.2 If a supervisor notes changes in the quantity or quality of an employee's work that may be related to personal problems, he or she may refer the employee to the Clinic Director for assistance, information and referral.

29.3 The Clinic Director shall review needs and provide the employee with referrals for service.

29.4 If an employee's performance does not improve after a referral for services, the supervisor may refer the employee back to the Clinic Director for assistance.

29.5 An employee's use of referrals shall not affect his or her performance evaluation. Performance shall be evaluated strictly on the basis of work-related issues.

29.6 All discussions concerning employee assistance shall be conducted in the strictest of confidence.

## Section 30 - EMPLOYEE SUGGESTIONS AND COMMENTS

Definition: Employee suggestions and comments are ideas offered to HAMILTON for consideration and action.

Policy: HAMILTON shall encourage suggestions and comments, which will: a) result in improved administrative practices, b) save time and resources, and c) improve programs and services.

Procedures: 30.1 Suggestions shall be provided in writing to the Clinic Director or the Operations Manager and may be submitted anonymously.

30.2 Suggestions shall be date-stamped and investigated by the Clinic Director or Operations Manager, or by an individual designated by the Chief Operating Officer.

30.3 If a suggestion offers possibilities but is incomplete, the employee who submitted the suggestion, if known, may be asked to provide additional information.

30.4 The employee who submitted a suggestion shall be notified of the results of HAMILTON investigation referred to in 30.2 above, provided that his or her identity is known.

## Section 31 - DRUG TESTING

Definition: HAMILTON is committed to a drug free work environment.

Policy: Accordingly, HAMILTON retains the right to test its employees for use when it has reason to suspect that said employee is using and/or under the influence of nonprescription drugs while at work, or the use of which during non-working hours is adversely affecting the employee's performance of duties. HAMILTON will make every effort to ensure confidentiality in the testing and reporting of results. Failure to submit to a request to undergo a drug test may be grounds for dismissal. Leave of absence and placement in drug or alcohol rehabilitation facility may be available for employees who test positive for drugs.

Procedures: 31.1 All employees will submit to a) pre-employment urinalysis prior to employment and, b) random urinalysis, c) reasonable suspicion - defined as supervisor observes appearance or uncharacteristic behavior that may be interpreted as a sign of substance abuse.

## Section 32 - SECURITY

Definition: HAMILTON's corporate security program is designed to secure and protect property and personnel from harm, theft and destruction.

Policy: HAMILTON shall maintain a viable and aggressive security system.

1. HAMILTON shall employ security officer(s) to monitor the facility and ensure that all patients and visitors sign into a security log.

2. All security officers will report directly to the Director of Security and Clinic Director.

3. All staff will obey the lawful orders of security personnel.

4. Security will be responsible for processing all incident reports and will be available to staff for security issues at all times.

5. All staff will sign for any equipment assigned to them. This equipment shall be kept clean and free of debris, scratches and damage. All computer equipment shall be covered upon leaving the facility at the end of the workday.

6. Any staff member that damages, defaces, soils, stains or breaks any office equipment will be responsible for replacing the original piece of equipment.

**FIGURE 13-2**. Complete Policies and Procedures Manual.

# Chapter 14
# Creating Primary Care with Pharmacotherapy Program

The fundamental purpose of this section is to provide in-depth detail on how to create an integrated environment in which direct access to both medical and behavioral services are provided in one facility. For those of you who are already running a pharmacotherapy program, and have chosen to create an integrated facility, complete information is provided to assist you with adding on a comprehensive primary care component to your present operation. The procedure manual will detail the patient flow that will be necessary for you to receive reimbursement for medical and pharmacotherapy services. The most important aspect of this program is that the primary care physician and not the addictionologist (physician specializing in pharmacotherapy) will control the patients' treatment plan. This physician will now work as a consultant on the case. The primary care physician will make the referral for behavioral treatment and thus becomes ultimately responsible for the combined care that the patient receives within the integrated environment.

## New Driver

The primary care component will be the new driver of your healthcare delivery system. The client that comes into your facility will now become classified as a medical patient whose entire treatment plan, which now includes medical and behavioral care will be under the supervision of their primary care physician. Normally, in most pharmacotherapy practices the physician that the client has access to is a doctor that specializes in detoxification. The medical treatment that is usually rendered comes in the form of an initial examination, and subsequent visits to regulate either a "holding" dose, or a scheduled maintenance visit. Through the use of this model your organization can provide direct internal medicine care, OB-GYN, pediatrics (age specific) and so forth. The specialties that you provide will depend upon the budget and the space that you have available. The physicians can work out of the space that you provide for them just like any other independent practitioner. Once they become members of your panel of providers you can bill for their services accordingly. In summary, the primary care physicians will monitor all medical progress; and, the psychotherapists will monitor the behavioral aspects of treatment. Additionally, as the principal of this new hierarchy, the primary care physician should by all means make appropriate consults to the staff psychiatrist.

## Significance of the Psychiatrist

A psychiatrist should always be on staff to provide ongoing behavioral healthcare for those patients that are presently taking medications who need to be monitored by a specialist. These high acuity comorbid patients (medically and behaviorally complex) who would normally see a psychiatrist in a "counseling only" environment will now have the benefit of receiving readily available primary care. For instance, bulimic patients who are prone to electrolyte abnormalities, esophageal ruptures, hypovolemic and carcinogenic shock, vomiting and diarrhea require close medical observation. Therefore, a comorbid patient who is being treated with a medication such as Prozac® will make an ideal candidate for this form of structured integrated environment. And once again, the psychotherapist will report regularly to the patients' doctor(s) as a required function of the interdisciplinary team.

## Disjointed Treatment

It is also reasonable to assume that these patients are several times more likely to be hospitalized due to historically neglected mental health needs, inconsistent, or inappropriate medical care, medical professional disappointment and disjointed treatment. Thus, you're going to definitely want to make sure that you have a working collaborative agreement in place with a local hospital for possible inpatient treatment.

Additionally, these patients normally will lack adequate access to primary health care, and will often have little, or no preventative medical care before they enter into this program. Patients who utilize the services of this integrated healthcare environment will be provided with primary care, substance abuse and mental health services as a bundled package. The fundamental concept here is to build an all-encompassing medical and behavioral community whose intended effect of action is virtually invisible to its constituents.

New patients that are currently receiving only behavioral healthcare services at other providers must have their treatment plans redesigned to include regularly scheduled medical services.

## Integrated Health Delivery System

The patients that this integrated health delivery system will benefit most are life long pharmacological and chronic illicit drug abusers. In general, the chronic drug abuser will have a Diagnostic and Statistic Manual (DSM) Axis I diagnosis of heroin dependence. Yet, other substance abusers whose choice of drugs include cocaine, methamphetamine, and alcohol will also benefit from this treatment setting as other forms of pharmacologic treatments such as Anabuse, naltrexone and L-alpha-acetylmethadol (LAAM), clonazepam, amantadme or desipramme will also be available. Given that there is a very large population of intravenous drug users who are capable of spreading a number of diseases such as HIV/AIDS it is of the utmost importance to mange their healthcare. Consequently, this group presents many health challenges that are extremely difficult to diagnose and treat.

Hence, the benefits of this model are abundant and present a unique opportunity to control the medical treatment of these patients. Characteristically, these patients are comorbid chronic substance abusers, sufferers of chronic mental health problems and members of low income and minority groups. Furthermore, this population is at an increased risk for many infectious diseases including AIDS/HIV due to the fact that they do not actively participate in preventative medical treatment.

## Catalyst For Compliance

The innermost significance of this model is it's initial ability to utilize the patients' physiological dependence to drive, and to keep him coming into treatment until he can become stable. The dependence itself becomes the catalyst for compliance. Moreover, patients who are admitted into the center for medical services should be screened for present signs of comorbidity. In view of that, a mental health professional should then refer those patients who are subsequently identified as being comorbid for medical evaluation. This should be done to achieve contiguous and consecutive treatment for each patient. Likewise, psychiatric patients with medical comorbidity must have treatment plans designed to treat both presenting problems conjointly.

All new patients that are admitted into the center should be assigned a primary care physician who is responsible for both their primary care and behavioral healthcare needs. The primary care physician is in essence the "gatekeeper" in the patients' treatment plan. It is important to note that any patient that chooses not to follow this recommendation should not be admitted into the center. It is also important to note that patients who agree to participate in this combined treatment model have pre-existing medical, behavioral and/or substance abuse conditions that may have inhibited, or interfered with the continuity of their treatment in the past.

## Facility License

The licensing and physical aspects of the program will be determined by your organization. But, generally your facility will need to be (1) licensed by your local and state board of health, (2) licensed by the Drug Enforcement Agency (DEA), (3) licensed by the Food and Drug Administration (FDA), and (4) zoned by your local planning office. The process of obtaining a new license is complicated and should be directed by a seasoned professional who is aware of the regulations and procedures that are in place at the time of your application. See figure 14-1 which is a sample checklist for the Food and Drug Administration (FDA) process.

## Sample FDA Checklist Guide

## CHECKLIST GUIDE FOR COMPLETING FORM FDA-2632

APPLICATION FOR APPROVAL OF USE OF NARCOTIC DRUGS IN A NARCOTIC ADDICTION TREATMENT PROGRAM.

1. Form FDA-2632 attached

2. Form FDA-2633 attached

3. N/A

4. N/A

5. Tentative schedule outlining (1) dispensing hours, (2) counseling hours, (3) hours to be worked by physicians, counselors, and nurses.

6. Goodwill Healthcare is a 501(c)(3) not-for-profit organization incorporated in 2004. The structure of the program begins with a board of directors, officers, directors and staff. This is the official chain of command as it pertains to the operations of the organization. Chart attached.

7. Presently, Goodwill Healthcare receives supplemental governmental funding. Patient fees and third party billing also fund Goodwill Healthcare.

8. Architectural plans demonstrate the dispensing, individual and group counseling capabilities of the facility. The facility is designed as a complete ambulatory facility that has taken into account all aspects of adequate capacity and operations of this program.

9. The number of patients that will be treated are estimated at several hundred per year.

**FIGURE 14-1.** FDA Checklist.

The process normally follows this flow: a) new construction, or renovation of existing space to be in compliance with state and local medical and counseling boards, b) local planning office approval of facility, and c) DEA inspection and certification. The DEA has to assign your facility a controlled substance number. In short, agents are going to come out to check alarm systems, storage safe(s), and do background information on the organization. Upon approval your DEA number can then be used to purchase methadone hydrochloride, or whichever controlled pharmaceutical that you are licensed for to use in your program.

# Wide-Ranging Guide

If you are already providing pharmacotherapy then you will just have to integrate the primary care piece into the program. The policies and procedures that follow (figure 14-2) are designed to incorporate many of the rules and regulations regarding HIPPA, security, and licensing board compliance. However, you are still going to have to customize this information to conform with the exact specificity of all the current requirements necessary to operate in your particular geographic region.

This procedure manual provides you with step-by-step guidelines in which to either enhance your current service process, or create a new program from the beginning. In it you will find provisions for admissions, billing, laboratory testing, appointments and so on. This wide-ranging guide should satisfy various licensing guidelines in many states. Upon the receipt of your application to provide this specific service, your primary licensing entity will send out the current requirements for licensure. At that point, a full comparative analysis can then be conducted. And, if you need to add, or delete certain sections to come into compliance, you certainly may do so at that time. Another important aspect to remember is that your physician (Medical Director) should be included in all discussions regarding these policies. For instance, he or she will definitely want to provide input regarding the outside medication control parameters that are found in the Medication Take Home policy figure 14-3. This policy should address the requirements for controlled and dangerous substances that are under the jurisdiction of the DEA.

## Handling Narcotics

The FDA will also stipulate to you during the application process its requirements for dispensing and handling narcotics. Before any approvals are made you must have your written procedures available for inspection and review. All written procedures must be in concert with the actual physical environment of the facility. Thus, if the policy indicates, "a patient must be at least 18 years of age" the patient's chart must contain proof of age. At some point in time, which will not be announced, an audit of these records will be made to ensure that no underage children have inadvertently been admitted into your program. One of the most important internal controls that must be vigorously monitored should be the admissions process. Again, in some areas due to demand, there could literally be hundreds of patients admitted into your program within a few weeks. The primary care model is specifically designed to ensure that all medical appointments are kept prior to the dispensing of any narcotic. Likewise, this guiding principle applies to every modality in the facility including alcohol and methamphetamine dependence. Again, these distinctive patients are historically medically noncompliant. This system of checks and balances ensures that the medical practitioner is proactively attending to the patient's comorbidity.

Hamilton Health Care, Inc. — Pharmacotherapy
Admissions and Operating Procedures

SUBJECT: ADMISSIONS POLICIES AND PROCEDURES FOR PRIMARY CARE, BEHAVIORAL HEALTH CARE AND MEDICALLY MANAGED PHARMACOTHERAPY SERVICES

Purpose: The admission procedures outlined in this policy are written to comply with state and federal regulations. The staff at Hamilton will adhere to this policy to ensure that all patients receive the highest quality of care. These policies are designed to provide staff with strict guidelines to assist our patients with reintegration into society through a primary care/behavioral health care environment.

I.      Primary Care Environment:

The physical environment and surroundings in which the patient receives treatment.

1. The atmosphere will be welcoming to the patient and conducive to medical treatment, including physically challenged accessibility.

2. The patient's right to privacy shall be enforced by all staff members.

3. Waiting areas, exam rooms, and counseling offices will be clean, well lit and decorated and furnished in an attractive fashion.

4. Reading materials related to issues such as HIV, substance abuse, sex, pregnancy, parenting skills and drug abuse prevention will be made available for the education of prospective and regular clients.

II. Personnel:

All staff, both clinical and administrative are responsible for providing direct treatment and referral services within an outpatient ambulatory setting.

1. The admission coordinators will be sensitive to patients' needs while conducting screenings and assessments.

2. All staff members will be familiar with rules and regulations, policies, services, treatment issues and other community resources for purposes of treatment.

3. All staff members will be culturally and gender sensitive, and reflect the demographics of the patient population being serviced.

III. Admissions:

The requirements and the process by which a patient is admitted for primary care or primary care with behavioral health care and/or pharmacotherapy.

## New Patients

1. Upon entering the facility all patients will sign the register at the reception desk.

2. The receptionist will give all new patients registration forms to fill out. Upon completion of the patient registration form the receptionist will call finance. Finance personnel will review the patient's insurance information or other method of payment. Finance will inform the patient of the amount of payment that will be charged for a particular service. Once the finance department has verified the patient's billing status, admissions will be called to commence the admissions process. No exception to this procedure is allowed.

## Current Patients

1. Upon entering the facility and signing the register the receptionist will check computer for verification of appointment. The appropriate care provider will see patients without an appointment with priority given to emergent situations. In the event that no emergent situation is occurring patients will be given the next available appointment.

2. The receptionist will then call finance for authorization for today's treatment and current payer status. Once finance has given the go ahead the receptionist will inform the appropriate provider of the impending appointment.

## Appointment Completion

1. At the conclusion of the appointment the provider will bring the patient, and the patient's chart up to the finance department for payment. No exception to this procedure is allowed.

*A. Primary Care*

1. Patients seeking primary care services <u>only</u> shall be referred to a primary care physician.

2. All patients requesting medical services shall have an appointment. The receptionist will confirm this 24 hours in advance. Walk-in patients will be accepted.

3. A medical assistant or nurse shall obtain patient vital sign information from the patient prior to his/her seeing the physician.

*B. Primary Care with Behavioral Health Care and Pharmacotherapy*

1. All patients requesting behavioral healthcare and/or pharmacotherapy will be <u>screened</u> by an admissions coordinator <u>prior</u> to referral to a primary care physician. No patient will be approved for pharmacotherapy services if they are currently enrolled in another program. This provision is designed to not permit multiple enrollments.

2. Patients requesting behavioral healthcare and/or pharmacotherapy must be examined and referred by a primary care physician <u>prior</u> to any behavioral treatment.

3. Patients requesting behavioral healthcare and/or pharmacotherapy must have a documented history of a minimum of one year of addiction to narcotics or opiates. All other substance abusers will be admitted as per physician recommendations.

4. A patient must be at least 18 years of age, but those patients between 16 and 18 may be accepted for services with parental consent and a documented history of two unsuccessful attempts at detoxification. This is essential to participate in any pharmacotherapy program.

5. An admissions coordinator will conduct a preliminary screening by telephone or in person to determine the patient's appropriateness for behavioral healthcare/pharmacotherapy.

6. Patients assessed as appropriate for behavioral health care and/or pharmacotherapy will be offered an appointment for a complete assessment.

7. The admissions coordinator will be responsible for referring inappropriate patients to other agencies more suitable to their needs. The admissions coordinator shall develop a list of referral sources for this purpose.

8. Should the center be at capacity, patients suitable for behavioral healthcare/pharmacotherapy will be placed on a waiting list, and may also be directed by the admissions coordinator to alternative treatment programs that can meet their needs.

9. Priority consideration will be given to pregnant women, HIV/AIDS patients, and those with other serious medical conditions.

10. Regulations affecting the confidentiality of drug and alcohol treatment, and medical records shall be explained to each patient by an admissions coordinator.

11. An admissions coordinator shall inform the patient that testing for infectious diseases, including HIV is voluntary.

12. An admissions coordinator will take a patient history beginning with the least stressful areas of questioning: demographic information, drug use/health, sexual practices and infectious disease.

IV. Screening:

Screening enables the staff to determine the appropriateness of a patient for primary care with behavioral healthcare and/or pharmacotherapy.

1. An admissions coordinator shall be responsible for initial patient contact at the time of screening. He/she will promote a positive relationship between staff and patient by being sensitive, caring and compassionate.

2. Patients will be screened and processed by an admissions coordinator. If a patient is deemed appropriate, he or she will be offered an appointment for a comprehensive assessment and medical evaluation.

3. Patients with special needs will be accommodated to the best of the ability of the medical center.

4. The screening process for behavioral healthcare and/or pharmacotherapy will include a complete psychosocial, and drug use history.

V. Medical Evaluation:

All prospective patients will undergo an initial medical examination before he/she receives primary care with behavioral healthcare and/or pharmacotherapy.

1. A physical examination for the presence of clinical signs of addiction will be performed by a primary care physician.

2. The examination will evaluate the observable and reported presence of withdrawal symptoms.

3. The examination will assist medical staff to diagnose infectious diseases in patients and provide a basis for infectious disease testing. The tests may include all or some of the following infectious diseases: tuberculosis, HIV, Syphilis, Viral Hepatitis A, B, C and D, gonorrhea, chlamydia, herpes simplex, and chancroid.

4. The examination will assist medical staff to plan and provide medical care for patients with infectious diseases.

5. The examination will provide a basis for preventive interventions and planning for follow-up care.

6. A complete medical history, including current information to determine chronic or acute medical conditions will be documented.

7. Any treatment the patient has had or is currently receiving will be documented.

8. Pregnancy, past history of pregnancy, and current involvement in prenatal care will also be documented. If the patient is not sure she is pregnant, a pregnancy test will be given as a precaution.

9. Documentation on the patient's family, including sex and date of birth of children, residence of children, and family medical history and drug use will be obtained.

10. The physician will make the final decision as to whether the patient is appropriate for behavioral healthcare and/or pharmacotherapy and will order the most appropriate method of treatment.

11. The admitting physician will inform patients of the results of the medical evaluation. The physician will explain the treatment process and treatment options. He or she will also explain the chances for success or failure and the benefits and risks of proposed treatments.

VI.     Informed Consent:

In order to participate in primary care with behavioral healthcare and/or pharmacotherapy, patients must sign an informed consent.

1. All forms and consents requiring a patient's signature will be explained to the patient.

2. The patient is entitled to be advised of his/her rights and responsibilities regarding confidentiality, health center policies and procedures, and treatment services.

3. Consent to treatment will be obtained from the patient on the FDA form 2635 (7/93), which affirms the patient's voluntary consent to receive pharmacotherapy as prescribed by the physician for treatment.

4. The patient will also sign release forms giving his/her consent to the center obtaining records from hospital and other agencies from which treatment was received.

VII.    Readmission:

Patients wishing to be re-evaluated once discharged from primary care with behavioral healthcare and/or pharmacotherapy will be entitled to the same rights, responsibilities and services as newly admitted patients.

1. The physician, executive director and counselor will review patient's previous involvement with program and accomplishments

in treatment. A patient's previous attendance record, reasons for discharge, and prior commitment to treatment will be reviewed, as well as, his or her cooperation with health center policies, and length of absence from treatment.

2. Patients will not be re-evaluated prior to 30 days from date of discharge.

3. Patients discharged a second time will not be re-evaluated prior to 60 days from date of most recent discharge.

4. Patients re-evaluated more than 90 days from date of discharge will repeat the entire admission process including the initial screening and physical examination.

5. Patients discharged for offensive language and/or violent behavior toward staff or patients will not be eligible to continue treatment.

6. Patients discharged for selling or diverting medication will not be eligible to continue treatment.

7. Patients discharged for violations of the "Patients Responsibilities" agreement shall not be eligible for continued treatment.

VIII. Patient Orientation:

All patients will receive a thorough and easy-to-understand orientation regarding key aspects of treatment.

1. The orientation will review the center's philosophy regarding dependence on narcotics and other substances. The counselor assigned to the patient shall be responsible for completing the orientation.

2. The counselor will describe the various treatment options provided by HAMILTON, hours of operation, medical services available and behavioral services offered.

3. A physician will educate the patient on the pharmacotherapy deemed most appropriate for his/her addiction. This will include dosage and side effects, medication procedure, responsibility in ingesting medication, take-home policies, and bottle return policies. The patient will also be educated on the procedure for requesting medications for travel or emergencies, security and proper storage of pharmaceuticals at home.

4. The counselor will discuss the patient's responsibilities when he/she has entered treatment, which will include participation in developing a treatment plan, working towards treatment goals, and attending both individual and group sessions.

5. Patient rights will also be reviewed by the counselor with the patient once admission into the program has been approved by the admitting physician.

6. Patients will be advised by the counselor that <u>under no circumstances</u> will medication be delivered to the patient.

7. HAMILTON policies and procedures for the center regarding discharge, loitering and take-home medication will also be reviewed by the counselor with the patient during orientation.

IX. Discharge:

Patients will be discharged from treatment at the discretion of the physician and director.

1. Patients who do not completely adhere to treatment guidelines because of the inability to commit to treatment will be discharged.

2. Patients who continue to use alcohol and/or other drugs will be discharged.

3. Patients who use offensive language or exhibit threatening behavior towards staff or other patients will be discharged from the program.

4. Patients who exhibit indifference towards treatment and who are not active participants in treatment will be discharged.

5. A written statement will be provided by the counselor as to the nature of the discharge.

6. Patients will have the right to request a review of the discharge decision by the program director. Patients may seek the advice from an outside source in preparation for the review.

7. Patients discharged from treatment will be referred to appropriate treatment alternatives.

8. Self-termination includes an absence of <u>three (3) consecutive days</u> or incarceration.

**FIGURE 14-2**. Pharmacotherapy Policies and Procedures.

*Matt Hamilton, MBA, Ph.D.*

# Hamilton Health Care, Inc.
# Medication Take Home Policy

SUBJECT: Take Home Medication Policies and Procedures for Medically Managed Pharmacotherapy

Purpose: The take-home procedures outlined in this policy are written to comply with state and federal regulations. The staff at Hamilton will adhere to this policy as it ensures continuous quality care and efficiency in providing medical and social services. The patient without direct observation of a medical provider will consume these doses of medication. A patient will be eligible to be considered for take home medication providing he or she meets the following criteria:

I.   *Detoxification Take Home*

1. Detoxification patients receiving treatment for <u>alcohol, cocaine</u> and <u>benzodiazepine</u> addiction may receive one day's dosage during the outpatient process as per physician order. Each patient must submit a daily urinalysis to confirm that the medication is being taken in the dosage being prescribed by the doctor.

II.   *Methadone Hydrochloride*

1. For patients prescribed Methadone Hydrochloride there <u>must</u> be an absence of recent drug and alcohol abuse.

2. The patient has attended individual and group therapy, and has received medication on a regular basis.

3. There is the absence of serious behavioral problems at the health center.

4. There is the absence of known recent criminal activity, for example drug dealing, burglary or sexual assault.

5. The patient's home environment and social relationships have proven to be stable.

6. The patient has been in medically managed pharmacotherapy for the desired length of time.

7. Staff must be assured that take-home medication can be safely stored within patients home.

8. The physician will determine if the rehabilitative benefit to the patient derived from decreasing the frequency of attendance at the center outweighs the potential risks of diversion.

III.     *Factors Considered for Take-Home Medication*

The physician will consider several key factors when initiating or continuing take-home medication.

1. The patient has remained in treatment for a sufficient period of time. This period of time is outlined in the treatment policies and procedures.

2. The patient shows no signs or symptoms of withdrawal.

3. The biochemical assessments in the past 90 days reflect the following results:

   a. Urine screen shows an absence of illicit drugs and the presence of medication.

   b. Blood serum medication levels are determined to have remained in the therapeutically optimal range.

4. The patient has no current untreated alcohol abuse or dependency.

5. Take-home medication will aid in the care of a patients concurrent medical condition.

6. The patient is in compliance with care for a concurrent alcohol, medical or psychological disorder.

7. Take-home doses will be appropriate in patient emergency circumstances, such as personal or family crises, bereavement or other hardships.

IV. *Factors Considered When Denying Permission For Take-Home Medication*

The physician will consider several factors when denying permission for take-home medication.

1. The patient shows signs or symptoms of drug withdrawal or continues to demonstrate illicit drug use as recognized by the physi-

cian, counselor or other staff members. In addition, biochemical evidence of an absence or suboptimal level of prescribed medication.

2. The patient is non-compliant with the treatment schedule for an acute or chronic medical or psychological condition, as determined by the physician.

3. No take home medication will be given out if the patient's character is considered to be unreliable, or irresponsible. Additionally, if the patient has presented staff with any evidence that he/she is clinically unstable and would be a high security risk, no medication is to be sent out with that patient until all concerns have been adequately resolved.

4. Security Hold. Security has prohibited this patient from receiving controlled take home medication.

5. No patient with a daily dose over 100 milligrams will be allowed take home privileges regardless of length in treatment.

**FIGURE 14-3.** Medication Take Home Policy.

# Chapter 15
# Organization Command and Control

There may become a time when your organization becomes bogged down in a financial or operating crisis. This situation can happen for many reasons. Such as an unanticipated and imminent withdrawal or suspension of a substantial amount of operating funds. This type of devastating funding shortfall can, and if immediate steps are not taken—close your doors forever. In spite of that, if you have already been in business for more than one year your chances for recovery are considerable. Then again, this is provided that you are prepared for a no nonsense introspection of your operation.

## SWOT

Conversely, your business may not be in an immediate cash shortage situation. Yet, on the other hand, you may not be content with the way that the business is currently operating. In either case, in order to get to the root of the problem or problems, a thorough "Strengths Weakness & Opportunities Analysis" (SWOT) should be conducted (see figure 15-1). First of all, this surgical analysis should be conducted by someone that is not involved in your day-to-day struggle to survive. Why? Often times when we are working 7 days a week to make things work out, our capacity to be objective is greatly diminished. Thus, it is necessary for someone whose advice is both trusted and respected take a look at the company from a higher altitude. In other words, you will need a fresh perspective of your situation. Normally, chaos progresses exponentially. That is to say, success has many parents and failure is an orphan. Moreover, in most situations where the financial strength of a company has diminished, a negative ripple effect on its operations occurs.

## Just Do Yourself A Favor

The slide downhill is often precipitated with several entities coming at you all together. For example, your funding has been slowly dissipating over a period of several months, which has resulted in an inability to pay vendors in a timely manner. On top of that, as fast as cash comes in, it goes right back out—seemingly without any long-term benefits. The enormous liabilities of the organization that were brought on by a lack of cash are now devastating its remaining assets. And, now given that the overall liquidity of these assets are meager compared to a mounting debt—how are you going to answer a reporters' phone call that wants to talk about a payroll story?

Well, it can be done. If you are presently in this situation, just do yourself a favor, and take a moment to remember the specific reasons that you are, where you are, in the first place. For the most part you cannot go back to the past, but if you're smart you will not dwell on the present situation either.

The key to coming out of this predicament is to humbly ask for all of the help that you can get. The one thing that you have to remember is that your organization has helped many people during the time that you operated under good circumstances, and all the while you were going through a difficult period. The good citizens of the community will remember this and ultimately come to your aid.

## Make Adjustments

Yet, before a correction can be made to alleviate this state of affairs an extensive review has to be conducted. The goal of this review is to produce a foundation in which a sound strategy can be formulated. There are three distinct sections of the analysis: 1) *Description of the situation* – this is where you are going to outline the brutal realty of exactly what ails the organization, 2) *Mission Statement* – this section describes your reason for existence and how the organization views itself and 3) *Situation Analysis* – a comprehensive breakdown of how the organization functions and interacts at every conceivable level is illustrated in painstaking detail. Once this process is complete you can move forward with the appropriate strategy selection.

The subsequent choice of the strategy is driven by the data that is collected and analyzed. Lastly, the most important point to remember is that once you begin a certain strategy you can make adjustments as the environment dictates, but do not abandon your strategy. The outcome will be positive if you can follow your plan with energy and consistency. Also, make no mistake about it you are a strong leader; yet, there are often times when you must continually motivate yourself—even when others are telling you to quit. So after your analysis is complete, do not hesitate to get right down to work. And, by all means do not expect a drastic change overnight, but, the mere fact that you are still in business will be a powerful testament to your will to succeed.

Matt Hamilton, MBA, Ph.D.

## **Sample SWOT Analysis**

Strengths Weaknesses Opportunities Threats (SWOT)

Company: *Revelation Health Care, Inc.*

Date: August 14, 2006

1. DESCRIPTION OF THE SITUATION

Revelation Health Care Incorporated is a not-for-profit organization that had reached a strategic reflection point in January of 2004. The company was propelled into a chaotic and tumultuous reformation of its business.

As a not-for-profit 501(c)(3) organization it had relied on the County of Emerald City to fund its entire operation. The County withdrew all of its funding due to both political, and company manifested problems. The company has survived for ten (10) years with intermittent government funding and its ability to generate revenue from ongoing operations. The political and internal problems that have plagued the firm for the past 10 years have been resolved. The County has recommitted resources to the organization; however, the funding is only ten percent (10%) of previous yearly funding. The operant question is—where do we go from here?

2. MISSION STATEMENT

a) Customer-market: To provide access to quality healthcare for low and moderate-income earners. We have a responsibility to the mothers, children, men, doctors, nurses and patients and others who choose to use our services.

b) Product-service: Our principal services are medical examinations, immunizations, preventative medicine, laboratory testing, psychiatric screening and counseling, substance abuse screening, testing and counseling.

c) Geographic domain: Our resources are dedicated to compete within New York State.

d) Technology: We use the most up to date medical and computer equipment on the market. This ensures that we can compete at the same level with larger competitors.

e) Concern for survival: We are well organized to operate our business prudently so that we can generate the growth and profits to further perpetuate our existence.

f) Philosophy: We are committed to providing culturally sensitive and quality health care throughout Hunterdon County.

g) Self-concept: Revelation is a relentless corporation that has a diverse team of professional managers, and intangible assets such as staff members who believe in our corporate vision.

h) Concern for public image: We are concerned and responsible for the good citizens of the community that we operate and live in. We are determined to improve the quality of life in general within our community.

**LONG TERM OBJECTIVES:**

1. Maximize shareowner value over time.
2. Increase Revenue to $1,000,000 or better by FY 2010.
3. Increase Company profitability 15 - 20 percent steadily over the next 5 years.
4. Competitive Position - REVELATION seeks to have more patients per physician in our market.
5. To be known as the premier health provider in the community.

3.  SITUATION ANALYSIS

A.  **External Environmental Analysis**

1) *Industry analysis*: the boundaries of the outpatient health care industry begins with performing basic medical exams, periodic testing and screening, preventative health care, immunizations, nutrition and dietary counseling, diagnostic x-rays, dental care, vision care, home health care and ends with pharmacy services.

REVELATION competes in a dual market, which is unique in that it has a license for two (2) primary functions. The first is primary care, which has been outlined above, and the second is drug treatment. The drug treatment industry boundaries are substance abuse counseling, psychiatric counseling and testing, and urinalysis.

The industry structure is as follows: (1) concentration - there are several hospitals, three Federally Qualified Health Centers (FQHC) and numerous stand-alone physician practices. Our geographic area is highly concentrated, (2) economies of scale - the hospitals do not enjoy this economy, as they are traditionally infamous for the high prices that are charged for their services. The FQHCs are limited to medical treatment and the independent physician practices are not staffed with superior management, (3) product differentiation - for the most part the competitors in the area have not clearly defined their products, there are perceived differentials that exist which have been around for years, however, no one competitor has taken definitive leadership in this market and (4) the barriers to entry in this market is extremely high; the cost for medical equipment is exorbitant and medical staff fees are very costly.

2) *Operating environmental analysis*:
a. Competitive position - the variables that should be included are market share, breath of product line, proprietary and key-account advantages, price competitiveness, advertising and promotion effectiveness, location and age of facility, capacity and productivity, experience, financial position and caliber of personnel.
b. Customer profiles - the firm should gain an understanding of their customer by examining the profiles that are shaped by looking at the following variables: geographic, demographic, psychographic, and buyer behavior.
c. Suppliers - the company should take a close look at the relationships that they have with their suppliers, as these relationships will determine their long-term survival. As they provide a form of financing for ongoing operations.

d. Creditors - the availability of resources will be a determining factor in the organizations' ability to survive and grow. The type and amount of credit available to the firm will determine the organizations' ability to make profits.

e. Human resources - a company must be able to attract and keep experienced and skilled personnel. There are several factors that contribute to the ability to maintain key personnel. (1) Reputation - a company is more likely to attract good personnel based on it s reputation and standing in the operating area, (2) employment rates - depending on the operating location there may be skilled workers available if other similar organizations have made layoffs and terminations, and (3) availability - employees that are not available within the area may be recruited, yet, pay and benefits must commensurate with the moving distance.

3) *Remote environmental analysis*: the external factors that originate beyond the company are not controllable by management, and occur irrespective of any strategic plan. The area in which we operate is poor and depressed. The social factors that affect us are many. There are many senior citizens. In addition, the state is moving towards making women on welfare work for their monthly assistance checks and many of them are now seeing doctors for the first time because of work requirements. The political factors that previously had a negative affect on us have began to change for the better. We have accumulated political support in our efforts to give and promote health care. The current political debate on drugs has

also opened the door for opportunities to request funding for drug treatment. There doesn't seem to be any technological changes in the background that will affect our ability to provide health care, as we are not in the medical technology development market. There are no ecological consequences associated with our operations.

B.     **Internal Environmental Analysis** - this is defined as matching the organizations' internal strengths and weakness to those opportunities and threats within the environment. The correct analysis of these factors will enable management to create a sound strategy.

<u>S W O T Analysis</u>:

*Strengths* - REVELATION has a strong community presence. We are accessible to many individuals and families that will not go to other traditional institutions. REVELATION has strong links with other community organizations that will provide referrals and marketing assistance. REVELATION also has many professional organizations' ready to provide superior technical assistance in finance, law and public relations.

*Weaknesses* - REVELATION does not have the financial resources to compete should a competitor choose to challenge our market share directly. Our image has a certain degree of negative connotations attached due to negative newspaper publicity. However, REVELATION does have a certain degree of respect within the community, because of its strong grass roots efforts. The organization has very poor financial ratios especially current ratio. The debt to equity ratio is extremely high. And, the gross profit margin is non-existent.

*Opportunities* - There are many low and moderate-income earners within the community that do not have a cohesive health prevention plan. Many individuals and families have not experienced proper medical treatment. Most of these individuals have been signed up by various MCOs.

*Threats* - There are several major hospitals in the area that are interested in controlling these lives. There are also three FQHCs in the area. There are several established physician practices that have been around for years. Fee for service has almost become extinct. HMO's control almost all forms of payment. Additionally, all mental health services that are currently paid by the states will be controlled by MCOs in just two years.

a) Major issues - Developing the ability to generate revenue that will support current operations without depending solely on government funding.

b) Competitive forces - At this time the barriers to entry are so high that there are very few new entrants into this market. At the present time the hospitals are the dominant leaders in this market. Yet, their costs are a major disadvantage to their competitive positions.

c) Key success factors - The key success factors are as follows: a retrenchment needs to take place that addresses financial stabilization, cost reduction, and strengthens internal systems.

d) Principal actors - the list is as follows:
- County of Hunterdon
- Various physician practices
- Established FQHCs
- Other social agencies providing the same or similar services
- REVELATION management

4. <u>STRATEGY SELECTION</u>

Due to the fact that REVELATION is in a severe financial situation the options that are available are limited, they are as follows:

- Turnaround
- Concentrated growth

These options are best suited for this organization for several reasons. The company has a weak internal control system. For instance, this non-profit has a historical inability to financially sustain highly trained personnel. In addition, the company is not financially stable. The only way to address this problem is through retrenchment that includes the continued development of operating polices, development of economies of scale and ruthless cost cutting. The organization definitively has a turnaround situation that is considered to be at a high level. This organization must stabilize immediately.

And, with that said, the organization has survived under many harsh, aversive and unforeseen internal and external threats. This is reason to believe that management can make a successful turnaround. Once, the turnaround is complete, a concentrated growth strategy should be implemented. This strategy should address the organizations' internal weaknesses in a rapid growth market.

Furthermore, the organizations' core competencies include their ability to promote themselves to their particular customer and they have a keen knowledge of buyer behavior. Additionally, the firm operates within a fragmented market where there are no true leaders.

**FIGURE 15-1.** SWOT Analysis.

# Summary
# For Directors Only

The non-profit counseling organization is an essential resource that should be available to all communities. This is usually the central place where many of the thousands of men, women and children who live in both urban and suburban neighborhoods receive their behavioral and medical healthcare. Historically, the Federal government has recognized this trend and accordingly has set aside millions of dollars in funding to address many of the issues directly related to inadequate healthcare delivery in these neighborhoods. This need has created a tremendous opportunity to deliver specialized niche services to these patients.

Many of you who are ready to go out and start a new practice will find that the community will welcome you with open arms. This will be the case whether your agency provides psychotherapy, or a combination of services, which may include a medical component. The mere fact that the integrated healthcare delivery system provides a one-stop shop for comprehensive healthcare under one roof makes it a very attractive model. And, for the organization that is currently contemplating the creation of a pharmacotherapy delivery system, this book contains all of the information that is needed to put together a comprehensive proposal and successful operating system. It was the intent and purpose of this book to provide you with the tools in which to create, operate and upgrade your own ideal organization.

# Index

## A

Absence 224, 234
Abuse 108, 146, 201
Access 112
Accident 207
Account 90
Accounting 78, 84
Accounts 84, 90
Active 133, 209
Administrative 87, 88, 90, 92-94, 183
Adults 35, 36
Advance 94, 95
Affirmative Action 166, 167
Agency 53, 55
Agreement 53, 115, 125-132, 138
AIDS 37, 51, 53, 147, 148, 149, 150, 151, 250, 251, 262
Airspace 100
Alcohol 35, 36, 37, 106, 150
Ambulatory 29, 124
Anabuse 250
Analysis 23, 143, 146, 153, 274, 276, 278, 280, 283, 286
Annual 53
Applicable 53, 235
Apply 127
Appointment 133, 260
Approval 94, 207, 211
Area 29, 144
Assessment 68
Assistance 135
Attempting 224, 234
Attestation 108, 143
Audited 78
Audited Financial Statement 78
Authority 15, 301
Authorized 115

## B

Banking 90
Behavioral 260
Benefits 126
Bi-Weekly 93
Budget 25, 38, 55, 70, 71, 72, 81, 82, 234
Business 4, 20, 22, 29, 74, 81, 94
Business Acumen 4

## C

Capital 38
Cash 41, 76, 90
Cash Flow 2
Categories 55
CDBG 47
CDC 146, 152
CDL 110, 111, 113
Census Track 144
Center 60, 61, 63, 65, 66, 68, 70, 104, 141, 146
Certification 55, 139
Certified 55, 127
Channeling 19
Chart 84, 253

Checklist 253, 254
Chicago 108
Client 62, 233
Clinic 37, 125, 172, 183, 241, 243, 244, 246
Clinical 63, 66, 183
CME 126
Coalition 110
Code 10, 226
Command 274
Commercial Drivers License 110
Commingling Funds 42
Commission 139, 233
Communication 6
Community 31, 47, 60, 61, 63, 68, 70, 118
Community Development Block Grants 47, 60, 62, 63, 73, 81
Companies 105
Company 108, 278, 280, 301
Compensation 193
Competitive 280, 281, 284
Completion 55, 69, 260
Compliance 53, 109, 251
Comply 127
Comprehensive 60, 61, 63, 65, 66
Computers 81
Concept 31, 32, 54
Concern 279
Conduct 111, 113
Conferences 126
Construction 61, 69, 70, 71, 72
Consultant 55, 72
Consultants 38, 81, 177

Consumable 38, 81
Consumers 32
Contingency 71
Contractors 110
Corporate 87, 90
Corporation 10, 113, 128, 147
Cost 38, 53, 55, 69, 81, 192
Counseling 35, 36, 108, 117, 149, 155, 162
County 29, 30, 32, 60, 62, 73, 108, 146, 278, 279, 285
Creating 247
Creditors 282
Current 23, 44, 53, 259
Customer 278, 281

## D

Date 68, 108, 138, 278
DEA 252, 254, 255
Delivery 31, 250
Demolition 70
Demotion 228
Dental 65, 126
Department 48, 52, 61, 64, 65, 84, 88, 89, 106, 108, 111, 113, 133, 134, 136, 137, 139, 142, 143, 144, 146, 147
Deposits 90
Description 61, 86, 133, 146, 276
Detail 66, 157
Detoxification 270
Developer 61, 64
Developers 72
Development 31, 48, 60, 62, 63, 68, 72, 73

Diagnosis 35, 36
Disciplinary 222, 225
Diseases 152
Disorderly 233
Division 53, 133, 136, 137, 141, 142
Documentation 264
Dollar 79
Donations 38
Drug 35, 36, 37, 106, 108, 110, 111, 114, 146, 152, 153, 252
Drug Enforcement Agency 252
Drug Testing 110
DSM 250
Duties 125
Duty 208, 209

**E**

Economic Development 74, 301
Ecosystem 25
Educational 57, 139
EIN 13, 97
Eligible 127, 197, 205
Employee 92, 94, 97, 105, 106, 108, 110, 129, 171, 176, 177, 232, 243, 244
Employee Status 177
Employment 121, 122, 125, 132, 158
Encounter 35
Environment 65, 257
Environmental 72, 280, 283
Equipment 37, 38, 61, 71, 81, 85, 88
Evaluation 35, 36, 55, 263

Evaluations 179
Examination 111
Expatriate 142
Experience 53
External 280

**F**

Facility 29, 61, 65, 81, 108, 124, 133-137, 252
Family 35, 36, 76, 124, 142, 155, 208
FDA 252-255, 265
Federal 10, 11, 17, 47, 48, 50, 51, 53, 83, 105, 106, 108, 110, 121, 144, 287
Fee 104, 284
Fees 72, 94
Finance 78, 87, 89, 94, 259, 301
Financial 12, 68, 69, 82, 83, 183, 301
Financial Health 83
Financial Integrity 82
Foreign Medical Graduate 139
Form 11, 55, 253
Formal 218
Formats 22
Formulate 67
FQHC 280
Fringe 38, 81, 177, 193
Fringe Benefits 193
Funds 55, 73, 193

**G**

Geographic 279
Global 29, 37, 38, 103
Goodwill 38, 60, 62, 63, 64,

73, 253
Government 57, 142
Grievance 218
Group 35, 36, 58

# H

Harassment 169
Hardware 71
Healthcare 253
Health Profession Shortage
    Area 119, 121
Hepatitis 263
HIPPA 155, 157, 254
HIV 53, 149, 151, 152, 153,
    250, 251, 258, 262, 263
HMO 30, 32, 284, 301
Human 126, 146, 147, 282

# I

Immigration 119
Immoral 223
Immunizations 35, 36
Implementation 68
Improvements 37, 70
In-House 103
Incorporated 113, 278
Increase 280
Individual 35, 36
Industry 280
Information 8, 54, 87, 173, 195
Injection 150
Inpatient 35, 36, 37
Insurance 72, 81, 82, 126, 193
Intake 81
Integrated 65, 250
Intern 178
Inventory 89

Involuntary 232
IRS 10, 11

# J

Juveniles 35, 36

# K

Kindred 18

# L

Labor 123, 182, 204
Laboratory 65
Labor Attestation 123
License 29, 31, 34, 37, 38, 52,
    55, 60-66, 68, 70, 81, 83,
    84, 87, 94, 103, 108, 113,
    118, 119, 121, 124, 132-
    137, 139, 142-144, 146,
    147, 149, 182, 250, 257,
    260, 270, 278, 280, 301
Licensure Board 139
Loans 74
Lodging 96

# M

Mail 91
Malpractice 126
Management 39, 63, 90
Manual 84, 125, 158, 246, 250
Marketing 23, 24, 37, 99, 101
Marketing Strategy 24
MCO 44, 45, 46
Medicaid 29, 31, 32, 35, 130
Medication 255, 270, 271, 272,
    273
Medicine 119, 122, 124, 145
Merit 192

Methadone 270
Mission 124, 276
Modes 97
Monies 127

## N

Narcotics 255
Nepotism 236
New Jersey Law Against Discrimination 158
Niche 58
NIDA 146
Nurse 81

## O

OB-GYN 248
Observance 206
Operations 37, 171, 172, 183, 241, 244
Operator 64
Opportunities 23, 274, 278, 284
Organization 81, 139, 274, 301
Orientation 266
Outpatient 35, 36, 37
Overnight 45
Overtime 191

## P

Paid 116
Participate 135
Participation 208, 211
Patient 36, 253, 266, 267
Patients 31, 151, 249, 259, 260, 261, 263, 265, 266, 267, 268, 269
Pay 189
Payment 94, 95

Payroll 90, 92, 93
Pediatric 35, 36
Performance 177, 180, 243
Permanent 89, 177, 193, 196
Permission 197, 200, 272
Personal 76, 202
Personnel 55, 125, 158, 163, 164, 171, 258
Pharmacotherapy 44, 247, 257, 260, 269, 270
Philosophy 4, 279
Physical 111
Physician 81, 119, 122, 124, 125, 126, 127, 128, 129, 130, 131, 136, 138, 141
Physicians 32, 44, 201
Plan 20, 29, 60, 62, 63, 67, 68
Planning 1, 62, 68
Policies 158, 163, 177, 180, 246, 269, 270
Policy 87, 88, 90, 92-94, 157-164, 166, 169, 171, 174, 176, 179, 182, 185, 189, 191, 193, 196, 199, 202, 204, 207, 211, 214, 216, 222, 227, 228, 231, 236, 238, 241, 243-246, 270, 273
Positive Revenue Management 50
President 204, 219, 220
Prevention 146, 152
Primary 43, 60, 61, 63-65, 68, 108, 247, 257, 260
Primary Care 44, 60, 61, 63-65, 68, 108, 247, 257, 260
Principal 285

Private  97
Probationary  176
Procedure  85, 88, 90, 92-94
Procedures  76, 78, 87, 88, 90,
    92-94, 157, 162-164, 167,
    170, 171, 174, 176, 177,
    179, 180, 182, 185, 189,
    191, 193, 196, 199, 202,
    204, 207, 211, 214, 216,
    222, 227, 228, 231, 235,
    236, 241, 243-246, 257,
    269, 270
Program  44, 55, 66, 110, 158,
    164, 193, 247, 301
Project  37, 55, 62, 68, 70, 72
Projected  36, 62
Promotion  192
Property  88, 89
Proposal  60, 63
Provisions  131, 210
Prozac  249
Psychiatrist  248
Psychotherapy  35, 36, 117, 155
Public  109, 182
Purchase  84, 85, 88, 240
Purpose  257, 270

## Q

Qualified  280

## R

Rate  35
Receipts  90, 91
Received  212
Reconciliation  91
Records  92, 148, 173
Recruiting  119

Referrals  35, 36, 37
Regarding  55
Registration  94
Regulations  108, 262
Reimbursement  95, 96, 97,
    212, 213
Release  87
Remote  282
Rentals  81
Report  214, 215
Reports  93, 215
Representative  115
Reserve  209
Resilient  71
Resources  126
Responsibilities  133, 266
Responsibility  88, 155
Restricted  41
Revelation  278, 279
Revenue  10, 40, 66, 280, 302
Revenues  38
Review  147
Revised  81, 165

## S

Safety  241
Salaries  27, 38, 81, 191
Salary  126
Sales  110, 112
Schedule  55, 68
Screening  262
Screenings  35, 36, 37
Script  103, 104
Security  81, 183, 246, 273
Selection  69
Services  52, 53, 55, 65, 66, 82,
    105, 106, 108, 110, 118,

142, 146, 147, 149
Sexual 169
Sick 126, 199, 200
Site 70
Sources 55, 73
Space 38, 81
Staff 127, 130, 131, 133, 135, 136, 137, 234, 271
Staffing 116
Statistical 29
Status 176, 177, 178
Stolen 88
Strategy 34, 62
Strengths 274, 278, 283
Structure 10
Student 177, 178
Subject 257
Submit 53
Substance 35, 36, 118, 146, 149
Substance Abuse 35, 36, 118, 146, 149
Suggestions 244
Summary 22, 38, 55, 60, 287
Supervisors 92, 216, 217
Suppliers 281
Supplies 38, 81, 85
Survey 72
Suspension 55, 227
SWOT 274, 278, 286
Syphilis 263
System 65, 66, 81, 84, 250

**T**

Take-Home 271, 272
Tax 11
Technical 49, 62, 63, 67, 68, 72
Technical Assistance 49

Technology 279
Telemarketing 103
Telephone 81, 104, 301
Temporary 89
Termination 231, 232
Terms 53
Testing 31, 106, 108, 109, 115
Therapist 81
Therapy 35, 36
Threats 278, 284
Training 81
Transfers 89
Transportation 97, 106, 108, 111, 113
Travel 38, 81, 94, 95, 215
Treasurer 19, 87, 90, 172
Treatment 53, 108, 146, 249
Trips 96

**U**

Unemployment 193
Union 110
Unit 53, 70
Unrestricted Money 40
Unsolicited 174
Urine 35, 36, 111, 114, 272
Utilities 70, 81

**V**

Vacation 126, 196, 197
Vacation Leave 196
Verbal 87, 175
Violations 223, 234
Visa 119
Volunteers 117, 178
Vouchers 95

# W

Wages 189
Waiver 142, 146, 153
Weaknesses 278, 283
Welfare 31, 32, 35
Witness 208
Working 69, 226

# About the Author

Matthew Hamilton, MBA, Ph.D.

Matthew Hamilton has over 15 years of solid professional experience in the healthcare field. During the divestiture of the Bell Telephone Company in the mid-eighties, he worked as a consultant to AT&T on one of the first Health Maintenance Organization (HMO) projects in the United States. He has held a variety of executive positions including Chief Operating Officer, Chief Financial Officer, Finance Director, Director of MIS and Program Director at several large hospitals and not-for-profits. He has been directly responsible for the supervision of construction and licensing for a variety of facilities including ambulatory care and hospital inpatient programs with multi-million dollar budgets.

As a financial healthcare consultant who specialized in accelerated revenue generation, Matthew has worked for Robert Half International and KPMG as a sub-contractor. During his work on various projects, he developed operational methodologies including organic data mining that led to the recovery of millions of dollars in revenue.

He has hosted seminars on the on behalf of the Economic Development Authority of New Jersey for small business owners. As a not-for-profit administrator, he has received awards as a field instructor for several nursing, teaching and community colleges in New Jersey.

He received a bachelor of arts in psychology from Rutgers University. His master's of business administration and doctorate of psychology were awarded by Preston University. He is also a graduate of the Cittone Institute with a major in computer programming.

In addition to this book, Matthew Hamilton has authored several widely read healthcare related articles published in *HealthLeaders Magazine* including *Predicting Nursing Turnover*, *Provider Strategies for Accelerated Revenue Generation* and *Why Hospital Leaders Need to Think Like Payors*.

Printed in the United States
37269LVS00003B/34